The Green Book

Of

Psychic Development

Understanding The Psychic Journey

By

CB Bjork

Acknowledgements:

I must thank God for showing me a path that allows me to connect to His divine love.

I also recognize my Guides, Angels, and Masters who have assisted my growth.

I would like to thank the following teachers who have helped me on my journey:

John Tolle

Sylvia Niehaus Strong

Jeffrey Poe

Mary Bannon-Poe

Maria Celeste Provenzano Cook

Kandy Kendall

I would like to give special thanks to my weekly development circle, Tammy, Diane, & Janet

Lastly, I am thankful to Janet for editing my gibberish into a readable tome.

Back Cover Photo By:
Andrew Alexander, Off The Beaten Path Photography

Contents:

Introduction

Welcome to a wonderful, strange, amazing, and enlightening journey. My goal in writing this book is to provide knowledge I gained as I went from someone who had no belief in psychic ability to working as a practicing, professional psychic. The time I spent learning and developing was quite confusing for me. I was unsure exactly what this ability was or how to determine if there was really something to this. I constantly had questions about what I was experiencing. I read books from many of the leading psychic/medium authors yet never discovered a detailed explanation of the process. For example, what is it like to experience clairvoyance, talk to your guides, or read tarot? I have written this book in an attempt to provide answers and insight to these and many other questions.

Throughout life I have discovered that the human condition is almost identical for all of us. Sensations, such as pain and joy, are experienced similarly for everyone. When we have a cold or flu, we have the same symptoms. In the physical world our human bodies share so many similarities, it only stands to reason that when we have a psychic experience it will be similar for each of us. How I experience clairvoyance, for example, should be very close to how you do as well. This is the foundation of this book. I will try to relate my experiences in such a way as to help you understand through my examples. It may not match exactly, but it may help you better understand your psychic abilities.

This book is not designed to be an all-encompassing book about all things that make up psychic abilities. That would be impossible! There are way too many parts of the metaphysical world to put into one book. I am not attempting to claim that this is the only way in which psychic abilities develop or work. However, many of the insights offered here will assist you in working with and further developing your abilities.

If you are at the beginning of your psychic journey, this book will help you recognize and strengthen your psychic abilities. If you are more advanced, this book is designed to provide insight into alternate psychic thought. Either way, the information contained within this book can be a handy reference for years to come.

I've never thought these gifts were given to me to hide, nor to selfishly use for my own enjoyment. I believe they were given to me to help others, to provide a service for people who need assistance. Should that help be a reading, a clearing, an explanation, or teaching, I have understood that it needs to be paid forward. What I have learned in my journey, I am sharing with you in this book. I have spent a lot of time seeking these answers and the truth of this strange yet fascinating ability. Maybe I can keep you from struggling as I have. Hopefully this information helps move you forward and allows you to have some wonderful and amazing psychic experiences of your own.

However far you wish to explore this interesting ability is entirely up to you. How fast you desire to develop is also under your control. This is entirely your journey and experience. I hope it is one that you find to be as fulfilling as I have.

Namaste,

CB

Spiritual Glossary

Since this is an introductory book, the glossary is in the front so you will be familiar with some of the terms used and their meanings.

Akashic Record - Also known as "The Book of Life." It is a record of all lives, events, and actions throughout time.

Angel - Divine messenger from the Spirit Plane who assists and protects us.

Archangel - High ranking, powerful angel from the Spirit Plane. Also works as a divine messenger.

Ascended Master (Master) - A spiritually enlightened being who was once mortal.

Astral Travel - Out of body experience during the dream state where the soul leaves the physical body, travels to distant locations, and has vivid recall of the experience.

Aura - Energy field that surrounds the physical human body. Often invisible to the human eye, but can be seen by some people.

Chakras - Spiritual energy points located in the human body.

Clairalience (Clear Smelling) - The psychic ability to obtain information using smell.

Clairaudience (Clear Hearing) - The psychic ability to obtain information through hearing.

Clairgustance (Clear Tasting) - The psychic ability to obtain information using taste.

Clairsentience (Clear Feeling) - The psychic ability to obtain information through feeling.

Clairvoyance (Clear Seeing) - The psychic ability to obtain information using your third eye.

Crossing Over - As a result of physical death, the soul leaves the Earthly Plane and goes to the Spiritual Plane.

Development Circle - Group of individuals who come together on a regular basis to work on their psychic/medium and intuitive abilities.

Earthly Plane - Having to do with a physical existence here on earth.

Ego - The part of the personal psyche humans use regarding thought and behavior and how an individual interacts with external reality.

Energy - Our original spiritual form. Used by psychics/mediums to connect to others, both physically and spiritually.

Enlightenment - A state of spiritual understanding and growth of the spirit.

Entity - Unevolved being that can be found on either the earthly or Spiritual Plane.

Energy Vampire - A person who drains energy from another without permission.

Ethics - Moral principles which guide people and their actions.

Ghost - The spirit of a person who has died, which has left their physical body and remains on the earthly plane.

Grounding - The ability to bring a sense of calm and relaxation to the self.

Higher Self - Our eternal, conscious self that is connected to the Divine.

Hit - Term used to describe when an accurate psychic information is received.

Karma - Belief that actions, positive or negative, are returned to us in kind, either in this lifetime or in another.

Lightworker - A person who works on motivating others to a higher consciousness, whose light is a beacon for spiritual beings.

Meditation - Process of clearing one's mind and relaxing the physical body to allow for communication and understanding of information from spirit.

Metaphysical - The study of topics related to the fields of psychic, medium, or extrasensory phenomena.

Protection - Also known as "psychic self-defense." It is the use of an energy form to protect from unwanted energy from another.

Psychic Tool - Any item that a psychic uses to obtain information. Examples are, but not limited to, Tarot, Runes, Crystal Balls, etc.

Scrying - The use of a crystal ball, mirror, or water to obtain images for psychic purposes.

Sentient - Finely sensitive in the ability of perception or feeling.

Sitter - A person who has come for a reading from a psychic or medium

Spirit - A person who has died and crossed over into the Spiritual Plane.

Spirit Guide - Being of the Spiritual Plane whose purpose is to help us on the earthly plane. Some guides are with us for a lifetime, while others are with us only for certain purposes.

Spiritual Plane - Where our soul should naturally go upon death. A non-physical dimension of energy where linear time has no relevance. The place where our masters, guides, and angels exist.

Systems Check - Checking the current state of one's body, feelings, and emotions.

Third Eye - Sixth chakra, located above the bridge of the nose and between your brows in the center of the forehead. Metaphysical center of clairvoyant sight used to obtain images.

Validation - Confirmation that information received during a reading is accurate.

Not Yet Awake

In your life, you may have had many experiences like what I relate below. Take some time to reflect on those instances of when you knew things but didn't exactly know why. You may discover that your psychic abilities have been trying to awaken inside of you for quite some time.

The first instance I recall was in 1987 when I was playing softball in a local park. An ambulance drove past the park. I watched that vehicle from the moment it came into view until it disappeared out of view. I knew that ambulance was significant, somehow it would impact me, but had no idea just how important it would be. A few hours later, when I got home, I discovered that the ambulance I watched had transported my father to the hospital after he suffered a stroke. This was well before pagers and cell phones were popular and I couldn't be easily contacted by my family. However, my spirit guides were giving me a big heads up that I didn't understand at the time.

Another instance that comes to mind was in the spring of 1991. Our neighbors were out of town when a spring storm passed through. I was returning home with some friends after shopping and mentioned to them that I thought something was wrong with our neighbor's house. As the friends were the ones responsible for watching the house, they tried to assure me that everything was fine. I shrugged it off, but couldn't shake the thought that something was wrong. A few hours later, I went to get dinner and when I came back, the same thought crossed my mind again. This time I decided to act. I went to check things out and discovered a tree had crashed through the back of their house. Their house was nestled into a very lush wooded area and the tree that came down did not alter the appearance of the tree line. In my untrained mind, I just knew something was wrong. I now know it was my guides who were trying to give me information. Unfortunately, these psychic experiences wouldn't be recognized by my rational mind.

Starting Out

"You must unlearn what you have learned."
Yoda – Star Wars-The Empire Strikes Back-1980

This quote provides a great foundation for developing and working with your psychic abilities. What you have learned in life about what is possible, what is true, and even what is, will be challenged and may be changed. If you are willing to open your mind to new ideas, new thoughts, new ways of *be*-ing, your psychic abilities will flourish.

When we are children, we are still attached to the spiritual. As we near the age of reason (about 7-8 years old) our minds start moving toward the physical and we forget our true spiritual selves. We become grounded in this three-dimensional physical existence. Our minds become attached to only that which is tangible or has physical form. To advance as a psychic you need to leave the rationality of this physical plane and reconnect with your true spiritual self.

In many respects, when your guides and angels work with you they will be working with the spiritual you, not the physical you. Meditation is a very helpful tool to reconnect with your spiritual self (your inner self, or Higher Self). It allows you to quiet the physical mind and reconnect to the true spiritual you.

Know that as you embark upon this journey, things will change for you. First, you will change. Because you are opening your mind to new ways of thinking, the person that you are will become more in tune with the person you wish to be. Second, the people around you will change as well. You may question some of the relationships that you have and may increase or decrease the time you spend with certain individuals. Lastly, you may notice that you have more freedom in positive decision making for yourself.

Are You Psychic?

Yes. That was too easy, wasn't it??

Have you ever thought about calling someone and then the phone rings and it's the person you were thinking about? That is an example of your psychic ability. The reason you don't have psychic thoughts more often is because you don't use that "muscle" all that much.

We all have psychic abilities because we all come from spirit. However, like anything you want to be good at, you have to practice. Yes, there are some naturals out there, but don't let that discourage you. With work, patience, and time you can get there too. Remember, being psychic isn't about an ego competition. The fastest way to fail here is to let your ego get involved. (There will be more on ego later in the book.)

Baby Steps

When starting out on this journey of discovery and growth, keep your expectations grounded. You are not going to be giving detailed readings anytime soon. Start by working simply and being able to have immediate validation. Practice with some of the games I have outlined at the end of this book. Start by trying to perceive simple pieces of information. For example, if watching out a window where people pass by, just start by discerning if the next person will be male or female. Don't start with "female, red jacket, blue slacks, dress shoes." Practice will make your abilities grow and in time you will advance to more difficult challenges.

Trust It Through

When you receive information from your guides, masters, and angels, you need to learn to trust it. Initially, it will be hard for your ego to not get in the way of the work. Your ego will try to convince you that what you get is not real or accurate. If there is any one principle that will help you succeed with your psychic or medium abilities, it is to "Trust it Through."

When you are doing readings for yourself or others, your ability to "Trust it Through" will be proven accurate time and time again. Learn to meditate so you can calm the mind and remove unwanted thoughts. Develop control of your mind so you are aware when information is coming through. When it comes in, "Trust it Through."

Guessing Game

Starting out you may feel like you are just guessing. Since you do not fully understand the process of receiving psychic information, just go with it. Work on getting validation of your information, as this will boost your confidence and foster growth in your abilities.

As you develop and grow you will become familiar with how you receive psychic information. Pay attention to the way you receive information that is correctly validated, as this will lead you down the proper path. Just know that what you are getting is real. You are working a muscle that has been dormant for a long time. Work on keeping things simple and "Trust it Through."

Minor Victories

Early on in my development I was struggling with how exactly I pick up psychic information. My development group was working on obtaining simple information. We were trying to connect into other classmates' energies and determine who they had in spirit. For this particular class, we had a newcomer who was also a psychologist. At the beginning of the class, she advised us of her occupation, and was curious about what we were doing. She also shared that she found this stuff hokey, but was willing to give it a try.

As class wore on, the tone of her questions stopped being inquisitive in nature and turned negative. The instructor was doing everything he could to keep the class moving forward, but the regular students were becoming a little agitated with the situation.

During one of the exercises, I connected into her energy in an attempt to find someone in spirit to demonstrate the validity of psychic abilities. I told her, "You have someone in spirit. I feel he is a male, probably a father or grandfather with very strong energy. I'm getting the initials E. A. Can you verify any of this?" The lady responded "My father passed away several years ago, his name was Tony

Alexander. However, "Tony" was a nickname and his birth name was Eugene." The lady was impressed with my information and told the class that while she didn't understand how I did it, she had to admit that psychic ability was a possibility.

Our instructor said, "How could he have gotten your father's exact initials, in the correct order, without some kind of psychic connection? Information like that would get a gold star for the reading."

For the first time, I felt I had an understanding of how to connect psychically and draw information from another person. I trusted the information I received and gave it to the other person. This little exchange provided me a glimpse into my psychic abilities.

Always be a Student

Once you start down this path, learning will be a continual process. Whether it is self-discovery or learning about different things, you will always be a student. Try to keep an open mind. There will be times when you will be introduced to new thoughts which may be confusing. Some may even be almost incomprehensible. When this happens, it just means you're not quite ready to learn or understand those concepts.

When I first encountered a medium performing channeling, I was unimpressed. I did not understand what was happening, let alone how. I left the room thinking it was all a joke on those who were watching. A few years later I was fortunate enough to assist a friend who was doing a public presentation on channeling. Being able to be close by as her energy changed during the channeling process was fascinating. It became real and understandable for me. I had grown enough that it now made sense. Finally, the student was ready and the master appeared.

Always keep learning, discovering, and growing. You will be amazed with what you can learn and do. Your guides, masters, and angels will assist you on the road of discovery. Trust them and you will have a wonderful journey!

Spiritual Self

Psychic ability is a natural part of us. We are spiritual beings existing in a physical world. Our purpose for being here is to learn. We arrange our lives, lessons, family, friends, and exit points before we are born. We come here, live our lives, learn what we can and return to spirit. Each time here we grow a little more.

Psychics and mediums have a higher energy which allows them a closer connection with those who are in spirit. As Lightworkers, our connection to the spiritual plane feels amazingly normal. This connection is not strange or scary, it is actually quite comfortable.

Generally, psychics and mediums are very spiritual people, that is, they have a strong belief in God. While some may use a different name to recognize our divine creator, they are still acknowledging a higher power. Utilizing our abilities connects our physical selves back to our spiritual selves, which can help bring you to a closer relationship with God.

Perception and Reality

Many people have false perceptions about psychics and mediums. There is a common belief that they are frauds or charlatans because people do not understand the work they do. People have difficulty accepting a reality that is different from what they believe. Because beliefs form the basis of our being, those who believe differently from a societal norm tend to exist on the periphery.

Because I am unable or unwilling to perceive certain things, does that make them unreal? No. Just because I am unable to experience something does not mean I should discount your experience. As a man, I am not able to experience the pain of childbirth. Does it mean that the pain does not exist? No. People do not believe in psychic abilities because they have not experienced them. This does not make them any less real.

In order to grow your abilities you will need to trust your own perceptions. This will alter your reality from what it once was. Know and live your own truth.

Psychically Safe

You have made a decision to learn about using your psychic or medium abilities. As a result, you need to learn how to protect yourself and your energy. While you are working with your guides, they will help protect you from negative energy coming through from the spirit world. However, you can still encounter negative energy in many different ways. To be an effective psychic/medium you need to make sure you keep your energy clear.

My favorite psychic energy protection comes from medium John Edward, *"I surround myself in the white light of God's universal love and divine protection."* [Edward, J. (2010). *Infinite Quest.* New York, NY: Sterling Publishing.] With this you are calling in the highest protection from the highest source. It is a protection based in love, the strongest energy there is. When invoking this protection, you also need to visualize yourself being surrounded in the white light. While you are not creating a physical structure, you are creating a psychic energy one.

Here are examples of three types of protection:

Bubble - Imagine yourself in a clear bubble (kind of like Glinda the Good Witch from The Wizard of Oz). The bubble is all around you. You can use it to wrap yourself, a room, car, house, boat, plane, etc. This is the protection I use while repeating the phrase from medium John Edward. Whenever I travel by plane, I always surround the plane in a protective bubble of white light. I also use it at night to wrap myself, my bedroom, and then my house.

Shower - Imagine yourself in a shower of white light. In this case, the white light is cascading over you like a drenching bath. Your energy cannot be tampered with while utilizing this protection.

Mirrors - Surround yourself with outward facing mirrors. This reflects back the negative energy of whatever is trying to get to you. It leaves you in an area of your own personal space in which you are protected. This is a good defense against someone who is in your area and is very negative or disruptive to you. The negative energy being sent to you is reflected back to the sender.

As you see yourself surrounded by the bubble, shower, or mirrors, use the protective phrase cited above. When you are using it on another item, change the phrasing to fit the need. *"I surround this airplane in the white light of God's universal love and divine protection."*

When you work at raising your energy to communicate with spirit, you are increasing the brightness of your personal energy. As a result, beings on the Spiritual Plane are attracted to you. Your brighter light is also going to attract ghosts and entities on our physical plane. If you find yourself being awakened in the middle of the night with some frequency, it may be due to ghosts coming in and disturbing your energy while you sleep. To eliminate this, before you go to sleep wrap yourself in your chosen protection. Then wrap the room, and finally, wrap the building. Make sure you wrap it above and below.

Systems Check

Starting down the psychic path requires you to have knowledge and control of your physical body. You need to have a baseline measurement of your body and how it feels so you know when something psychic is happening to you. Being psychic means you recognize when you are receiving information.

Take a few minutes to sit or lie down in a place that is quiet. No phones, kids, television, or interruptions. Be there quietly and feel yourself from head to toe. Experience the sensation of nothing. This is your body at its baseline.

If you are sensing something energetically, there will be a different feeling in your body. Maybe it's a sensation of cold, or a tingle, or pain, or even hair standing on end. When this happens you can remember your baseline and know something is different. Now you need to ask yourself why this is different. Is there something in your environment that is causing it? Maybe the air conditioner is on and you're cold. If there are no outside stimuli causing the change, then what you are feeling is a true psychic event.

Ground and Center

Before doing any energy work, always ground, center, and protect yourself. These are the three most important things psychics or mediums can do when using their abilities.

Have you had trouble focusing on a project? Maybe difficulty remembering things? Feel a little scattered? Maybe you're angry for no reason. What is happening is that your personal energy is disrupted. Grounding yourself is a great way to bring your energy back into harmony. Centering yourself will focus your energy. Protecting yourself will keep other energy forms from attaching and causing you trouble. These practices will make you more balanced, focused, calm, and protected.

Here is what you do:

Place both feet firmly on the floor. It doesn't matter if you're in a high rise or boat or even a plane. Close your eyes and breathe in through your nose, hold for a second or two, and then exhale through your mouth. As you breathe in, feel roots growing from your feet into the ground. (Again, don't worry if you are not directly connected with the ground.) Hold that breath for a second or two, then exhale through your mouth. Breathe in again, and feel the roots go even deeper into the ground, hold for a second or two, and then exhale through your mouth. When you breathe in through your nose this time, feel the Earth's grounding energy move up through your roots, into your feet, and up your legs. Hold that breath for a second or two, and then exhale again through your mouth. Breathe in again through your nose and feel the Earth's grounding energy rise higher into your abdomen and up into your chest, hold it for a second or two, then exhale through your mouth. Breathe in again through your nose and feel the Earth's grounding energy rise through your arms, neck, and head, hold it for a second or two, then exhale through your mouth. You have just grounded yourself, but you're not done yet.

Now when you inhale through your nose, breathe in only positive energy from the air. Think of the air holding little positive (+) and negative (–) particles. You only want to inhale those +'s. Hold your breath for a second or two and when you exhale through your mouth send out all of the negative energy (–) in your body. Repeat these steps two more times, or until you feel all the negative energy has been removed.

Before you finish, surround yourself with your preferred method of protection and then open your eyes. You should be able to feel a difference in your energy and focus.

As you do the grounding exercise, you should be able to feel the energy rise up in your body. If you don't feel anything at first, do not give up. Remember, you are just starting on this journey. Don't be disappointed if at first you don't feel like you are succeeding. Some abilities will come on quickly, others will take time.

What you feel may differ from what I feel. I get a light feeling of pressure and can feel the energy tingle as it rises. Check yourself before you do this exercise and sense your body as you do this. Pay attention to the small changes. By the end of this exercise you should feel physically and mentally clearer and calmer.

Meditation

Meditation is the best method for learning to hear your guides and catch their advice. You spend a lot of time listening to yourself. Think of your mind as a swimming pool where the water represents all of your thoughts. In order for your mind to hear your guides, masters, and angels, they would need to dive through the water and touch the bottom of the pool. Meditation will help you drain the shallow end of the pool and allow them easier access.

Before you start any meditation, always ground yourself and then do your protection. While in a meditative state you are energetically vulnerable and especially so when you first start. Grounding and protecting are the two most important things to perform when you are doing psychic work. Calming and centering your mind will help you discern your own thoughts from those of your guides, masters, or angels.

Starting out by using guided meditations is helpful. Meditation will set the stage for your mind to clear, allowing an easier path for your spirit and your guides to make the connection.

As you sit down to meditate, after you have grounded and are protected, your next step is to eliminate your worries and concerns. Imagine a jar. Put all of your worries and concerns inside that jar, then screw the lid down tight. Once you have done that, mentally throw the jar as far from you as you can. Your worries and concerns are now locked far away and cannot bother you.

Like any other activity, you may struggle at first. Thoughts that are not part of the meditation will pop into your head. Because thoughts are energy, you need to acknowledge these thoughts and then move them aside. Many of these will come from your ego because the ego does not want to be quieted.

Breathing is an important part of your meditative and grounding work. Just like your grounding exercises, breathe in through your nose, hold for a second or two, and exhale through your mouth. This breathing technique helps to keep your mind quiet and focused.

Don't worry if during the meditation you lose this breathing pattern and return to normal breathing. The more meditation and breath work you do the better you will get at performing both of them together.

Meditation Tips

Are you a morning, afternoon, evening, or night person? It is best to meditate when your energy cycle is at its highest. Morning people should meditate in the morning, afternoon people in the afternoon, etc. Because your energy is at its highest, you will have an easier time connecting. If you meditate at a low energy point, you are likely to fall asleep.

The foods you eat can hinder your ability to effectively meditate. If you are eating processed foods with empty calories, your body is not able to use these as quality fuel. Eat natural foods that are not processed, more fruits and vegetables, and whole grains. Avoid caffeine, soda pop, and energy drinks. These may give you a physical stimulus, but they do nothing to assist your spiritual energy.

Chakras

A chakra is a spiritual energy center located within your physical body. There are seven main chakra energy centers in the human body. They are: Root, Sacral, Solar Plexus, Heart, Throat, Third Eye, and Crown. Each chakra has a different color, vibration, and purpose.

Each of us has a dominant chakra that we work with and a passive one that causes us concern. Our dominant chakra will help with how we see and act within the world. Should your Throat Chakra be dominant, you will be a strong communicator, and will speak your mind. Your passive chakra will highlight a weakness for you. For example, if your throat chakra is passive, you will be timid in speaking out, may prefer writing to talking, or even have health problems in that area.

Root Chakra – This is your first chakra and is located at the end of your tailbone or coccyx, centered between your anus and genitals. It relates to the color red. The Sanskrit name is Muladhara. It responds to the musical note "C". When in balance it promotes stability and harmony. When out of balance you may experience auto-immune disorders or depression.

Sacral Chakra – This is your second chakra and is located just below the navel. It relates to the color orange. The Sanskrit name is Svadhisthana. It responds to the musical note "D". When in balance it promotes healthy emotional connections. When out of balance, you may experience sexual dysfunction or digestive/bladder issues.

Solar Plexus Chakra – This is your third chakra and is located just below the breastbone. It relates to the color yellow. The Sanskrit name is Manipura. It responds to the musical note "E". When in balance it promotes personality and knowing. When out of balance, you may experience stomach issues or self-image issues.

Heart Chakra – This is your fourth chakra and is located at your heart. It relates to the color green. The Sanskrit name is Anahata. It responds to the musical note "F". When in balance it promotes healthy love and emotional empowerment. When out of balance, you may experience circulatory issues and feelings of guilt or anger.

Throat Chakra – This is your fifth chakra and is located at your throat, just above the breastbone. It relates to the color blue. The Sanskrit name is Vishuddha. It responds to the musical note "G". When in balance it promotes truth and self-knowledge. When out of balance, you may experience problems in the throat, thyroid, or jaw or inability to communicate.

Third Eye Chakra – This is your sixth chakra and is located above your brow, centered over the bridge of your nose. It relates to the color indigo. The Sanskrit name is Ajna. It responds to the musical note "A". When in balance it promotes insight and wisdom. When out of balance, you may experience problems with your mind, vision, and hearing.

Crown Chakra – This is your seventh chakra and is located at the crown of your skull. It relates to the color violet. The Sanskrit name is Sahasrara. It responds to the musical note "B". When in balance it promotes a connection to your spiritual source. When out of balance, you may experience problems with cynicism, confusion, or lack of purpose.

Your Clairs

There are five main clairs that match your five main senses: sight, hearing, touch, smell, and taste. The five matching clairs are: Clairvoyance (clear sight), Clairaudience (clear hearing), Clairsentience (clear feeling), Clairalience (clear smelling), and Clairgustance (clear tasting). Beginning psychics are usually aware that one of their clairs is active and that is how they receive extrasensory information. Your primary gift is the best way for you to receive information, don't let your ego diminish it by wanting other clair abilities. This isn't a competition, it's a gift. Work with your gift to make it the best that you can.

You have seen a ghost, does that make you clairvoyant? You can taste your Grandma's chocolate chip cookies and she's been dead for 17 years, does that mean you're clairgustant?

For the sake of this argument, the answer is no. Here is why. People with clair abilities use them as part of their daily lives to glean extrasensory information that they would not otherwise know. Just because you have seen a ghost or have a taste for your grandma's cookies doesn't mean you have fully developed clair abilities. What it does mean is that you have experienced something that will hopefully lead you to further develop the abilities you do have.

True clair abilities have a higher energy about them that allows your physical senses to detect information on the physical or Spiritual Plane. This helps you to see, hear, and feel with a clarity that the vast majority of people cannot fully understand. Working with your clair gifts will help you understand the information you receive and aid you in further developing your primary clair and adding others.

Clairs and Energy

Understand, it takes energy for those beings that are not physical to make contact with you. For them to always appear, or make sound, or create a sensation of touch is so energetically draining they can't contact you a lot. Therefore they must work with you in a way that is easy for them.

Think of your guides as existing at about 10,000 feet above the earth. They are trying to yell information down to you. You are doing all you can to see, hear, or feel anything coming from above; however, all the noise down here prevents it. But, what if they could come down some and you could go up some, wouldn't that help?

In essence that's what happens. They need to slow down their energy vibration and you need to speed yours up. As this happens, you get closer to them and suddenly their contact becomes clearer and more regular. However, they don't use our physical senses because that is too daunting, so they give it to us in an electrical sense. They stimulate our senses with their energy.

Clairvoyance –
Clear Seeing

True clairvoyance is a unique gift. True clairvoyance is the ability to see things that are not normally visible to the naked eye. Generally, it is an ability to see information with the third eye. Even among most psychics and mediums, it is a gift that usually has to be taught. So, if they can learn it, why can't you, right? While I have seen apparitions with my physical eyes, I need to use my third eye to pick up information psychically.

Your third eye is located about an inch or so above the bridge of your nose, between your two eyebrows. To activate it, take your index and middle fingers and gently rub in a circular motion in this area. Do this a few times per day.

Generally, when you start to get images you will not see them with your physical eyes. When your eyes are closed, look at the large dark screen in front of you. This is where the images are going to appear. At first, you may just get colors. Concentrate on them closer and you will probably discover some texture to those colors. With time and practice they will develop into shapes, then into recognizable items, like a car, a person, an apple, etc. At times, what you receive will be basic because that is all the understanding you need. Other times the images will be very specific. It doesn't mean only the specific ones are important, it means that some things can be communicated in a general way while others cannot.

When you are getting ready to go to bed is a great time to spend a few minutes working on your third eye. As you are laying there, ready to sleep, rub your third eye and then close your eyes and watch your private screen. Let the images flow naturally, don't try to control them. The more you work on this, the stronger your third eye will become. This is also good for having stronger visual dreams and being able to remember them.

Clairaudience –
Clear Hearing

To receive information that you would not otherwise know by hearing is clairaudience. When you are receiving information on a clairaudient level, it can be with your physical ears. However, most times it will be internal and only provided within your mind. This proves tricky to the person who is just learning about this skill or just discovering they have it.

When starting out, you may have a hard time picking up what is and is not clairaudient. Because this is gift is "clear hearing," I assumed it happened with my ears. As a student, I spent plenty of time waiting around for someone to whisper information into my ear. Alas, I was very disappointed. What I did learn, however, was that my guides, masters, and angels were happy to work with me clairaudiently. They did not whisper into my ears, but into my thoughts. The goal is to learn what thoughts in your head are yours and which are theirs.

Learn to quiet your mind during meditation and develop a focus so that your mind is only on one item. Then when a thought is dropped in, which is almost like a soft whisper into your thoughts, you will recognize it as clairaudience. The feeling is like a thought dropped into the center of your head.

Once you start developing this gift, remain open to receiving information at any time. As you go through your day, you will discover that your guides, masters, and angels will be working with you. It can be something small, like guiding you to drive down an extra aisle at the grocery store which results in a better parking space. It can be something big, like guiding you to take an alternate route home thus avoiding the 12 car pileup that happens on the interstate.

Developing this skill will prove beneficial when working as a medium, you will discover this is one of the best ways to get information from those who are on the Spirit Plane.

Clairsentience – Clear Feeling

Clairsentience can be experienced in a variety of ways. There are so many possible methods of sensing and feeling. Don't be discouraged if you process information differently than other clairsentients do. Sometimes you will feel something inside of you, like a shiver, cold, tingling, or possibly lightheadedness. Other times it will be external, a sense of an unseen presence, or a feeling of energy.

With clairsentient abilities, you should start by doing a full body systems check. You need to know how you feel before your clairsentience activates so you are aware when you are receiving information. Meditation is a great way to develop your clair senses. By quieting your mind, you will be able to better understand when your physical self is communicating clairsentient information.

Think of a time when you had a strong feeling about something and you didn't know why. What were you feeling inside at the time? Clairsentience as an internal sensation manifests in physical responses. Your body will give you signals that you need to recognize and understand.

Because your clairsentient abilities may work differently from mine, I can only explain this gift through generalities. I get a slight buzz feeling in my body when I am being provided with psychic/medium information. Yours might be a chill, a sense of cold, etc. What is important is that you pay attention to your body and its responses, don't ignore them. The more you work with them, the stronger you will become.

One specific I can give you as a clairsentient is this: When interacting with ghosts or spirits who have crossed over and they are showing you how they died (heart attack, gunshot, accident, etc.) you will feel it strongly because of your abilities. Tell the ghost or spirit to stop once you get the sensation, because it can be a bit painful – just like it's happening to you.

As a clairsentient you are also bombarded with external stimuli in the course of your daily existence. What other people are feeling, thinking, and experiencing will be picked up externally by your body as well. The majority of these sensations will come at you as energy arrows. You'll be hit suddenly with a headache, or become angry for no reason, because the person experiencing these sensations does not understand how they are shooting off their energy.

I used to enjoy taking trips by airplane. However, now that we're packed like sardines into a steel tube, the energy in a plane is more like a focused emotional energy missile.

53

There are people on the plane who are terrified to fly, scared of the take-off or landing, and freak out with a little turbulence. Instead of enjoying the flight, I now spend most of my plane time protecting myself energetically, and applying calming energy where needed.

As a clairsentient you need to be aware of how other people are affecting your moods, physical condition, and reactions. Again, being able to do a full systems check on your body from time to time will help you. The example above is just one simple example of how you can be affected. You encounter hundreds of people in a day and each one can leave their energy imprint on you. It's your choice whether to be influenced by their energy or only use your own.

Clairgustance –
Clear Tasting

This is the ability to clearly taste something when nothing has been put in your mouth. It is quite a unique gift to have and can be used in many different ways. It is a sensation that can be a bit overwhelming because it is tactile. While the other clairs are more thought or mind based, this one is more physical.

This ability is better suited for when you are working with ghosts or spirits who have crossed and they are trying to give you an exact sensation. If a spirit was poisoned, they may provide you with a chemical taste. If a grandmother is wanting to provide evidence, you may get to taste her apple pie. Each situation and its taste will be unique.

It can also be a handy tool for those who do psychic detective work. The spirit or ghost can let you taste things that are pertinent to their death. This gives investigators a better idea of what was happening at the scene of a crime.

This gift is literally just what it sounds like, clear tasting. You will be able to taste in your physical mouth a taste of the item presented. You can even have the sensation of something you have never eaten or drunk before. If you are giving a reading and information is presented to you in this fashion, you will need to describe what it is for the client. Because this information is relevant to the client, we must not exclude it just because we may not understand what we are tasting.

If the taste becomes overwhelming, you can ask your guides to remove the taste. If you need a glass of water to clear your mouth, that is fine. Do what you need to remove a taste that is unpleasant.

Clairalience ~ Clear Smelling

This ability closely mirrors clairgustance in that it is more of a physical sensation than the other clairs. This gift allows the user to smell a scent or odor clearly.

Clairalience is better suited for when you are working with ghosts or spirits who have crossed and they are trying to convey an exact scent. Examples could be perfumes, cooking, or possibly natural scents. You may be given scents that you have never smelled before. When this occurs and you are reading for a client, remember that the scent is for them, so describe it as best you can.

When performing a séance, it is quite common for a scent to fill the room. When the medium leading the séance goes into a trance, the scents associated with the deceased individual may appear. This is to be taken as evidence that the medium has connected with the person who is associated with that scent.

Because this gift is more physical in its nature, sometimes a scent may be too powerful or overwhelming. It is okay to ask you guides to remove the odor so it does not cause any harm to the psychic or medium.

Meeting Your Guides, Masters, and Angels

Starting out, your best opportunity to meet your guides, masters, and angels is during meditation. Once you have quieted your mind, you will be able to better hear them communicate. Initially, it is best to ask for signs to validate information from your guides, masters, and angels.

Let's say you wish to know the name of one of your guides. During meditation you ask "What is your name?" You then hear or get a sense of a name. The next step is that name must be validated by spirit putting a sign in front of you. It can appear quickly or it can take a few days.

Do not ask for overly simplistic or extremely difficult signs from your guides. They have to be given a chance to honestly respond. You also have to accept the signs they give to you. Let's say you ask for Mickey Mouse as a sign. Well then, if you see Mickey Mouse drawn on something, it's a hit. But what about if you go to the store and the person checking you out is named Mickey? Well, that is a hit too. Your guides, masters, and angels will provide information in different and interesting ways.

When You First Communicate

Throughout your whole life, your guides, masters, and angels have been providing you information that you were not aware of. Your first intentional communication with your guides and masters will be unusual because you do not know what to expect. Unless you already have well-developed "clair" abilities, your first contact will probably be a lot like mine - - confusing.

First, when your guides or masters make contact, it may be like a little thought is dropped into the center of your mind. It will be soft, which may make you question whether or not it was you thinking it or them giving it.

Second, don't try to overthink it. You need to become comfortable accepting what you get as being true. The information given may sound bizarre and be out of the ordinary, but if you trust it through, you will discover it is valid.

Third, if you are asking for the names of your guides or masters, don't expect to get Mr. John Smith. Your guides will be colorful. You may find that their names may be familiar, or they may be strange and unique. Be open to the experience.

Finally, recognize the subtle sensations you experienced before, during, and after the contact so you can be aware when it happens again. I initially had trouble recognizing and trusting the information. As time went on and it happened more and more, I became familiar with it. Now, my guides are with me everywhere and drop in all the time. You may discover that your guides and masters will provide you with information and comments throughout the day.

Remember to thank your guides when they provide information to you. They like to be appreciated just as much as you do.

Meeting a Guide

The first meeting with a guide can be frustrating for the student. Trusting the information that is provided proves difficult for many. This was no different for me as I worked on meeting my guide, Snoopy.

One of the best ways to meet a guide is through meditation. I knew my guides were there, I had heard their presence before, but I really didn't know any of them by name. As I sat down to do another guided meditation, I cast all of the previous failures aside in hopes that this one would be different. During the meditation, I heard a single word that came from a distant voice in the center of my head. It was very clear as it said, "Snoopy." I know that I must "trust it through" when getting information, but I wanted validation.

When you meet your guides, they will provide validation through the reasonable method you set up. This was to be no different for me. It's easy to think that as popular as the Peanuts character Snoopy is, validation would be a breeze. It took several days for Snoopy to actually appear to me, but when he did, it was with gusto.

There I was, flipping through Facebook, when an image of Snoopy appeared. The important thing was not that his image was there, it was the message included as part of the image. The picture was titled, "A Perfect Friend." As part of the image, such phrases as "full of great advice," "ready to listen on a moment's notice," or "always happy to see you," were included. To me it wasn't just a validation that Snoopy was my guide, but also of all the great attributes my guide has for me.

Respecting your guide is important. Snoopy only wants to be called "Snoopy." He does not want to be called "Snoop" or "Snoop Dog." When I make the mistake and use one of the latter terms, I can see his brow narrowing into a stern look of disapproval. Use the name they provide as it is as important to them as your own name is to you.

Free Will

As sentient beings, we have free will. We can make choices and act upon them as we desire. We are responsible for our actions. There are consequences to those actions. Some we reap instantly while others are delayed. Our ability to grow spiritually depends greatly upon using free will responsibly.

Free will follows us when we leave the physical world as well. When our bodies die, we can choose whether to remain here or move over to the Spiritual Plane. When the light appears, you can move into it or away from it. This is your free will at work. Remember, this choice also has consequences.

Psychics can provide you with a glimpse into the future, but you have the ability to change the outcome with your free will. Once you understand what lies ahead, you can let it come to pass or choose to change it, it's your free will.

Discovering My Energy

In July, 2001, I went to St. Augustine, Florida, for a long weekend. On my first night there, I went on a walking "Ghost Tour." After touring a number of locations, our group stopped at a little narrow cemetery with high walls and an iron gate. Our tour guide talked about how people on previous tours had seen ghosts and had their hair or clothes pulled at this location. After a couple of minutes the group moved on to the next location, but I remained behind. I wanted these "ghosts" to make an appearance to prove they existed. As I stood at the gates, peering deep into the darkness, I said to these "supposed" ghosts, "Okay, prove it!" The 85 degree Florida night suddenly got frigidly cold. It was like every hair on my body stood on end and I could feel a vibration inside of me. All of this freaked me out so I left the cemetery gates and quickly caught up with the group.

At the time I was working for a company setting up residential phone service when a woman called in to initiate service. While creating the account, I asked her what she did for a living and she kind of laughed and said, "I'm a ghost buster, I do psychic work." I related the story about what happened to me a couple of weeks earlier and she told me that I had a psychic ability called "clairsentience." She told me that I could feel when ghosts were around. Basically, clairsentience is the ability to sense energy. Without feeling and experiencing it, I would have never thought it possible.

Reflecting on this time in my life, I have come to understand that there were higher forces at work in my life. I was exposed to a situation which made me aware of my psychic/clairsentient abilities. Within two weeks, an opportunity was presented to me to meet a psychic medium who could tell me about what I experienced and explain to me what it was and why. I then went on to have other clairsentient episodes which reinforced that initial experience. I was being guided by a larger hand to a new way of thinking and viewing life. As my understanding of energy changed, so did I.

Energy

The Law of Conservation of Energy states that energy cannot be created or destroyed. It can only be changed from one form to another.

Your physical body acts as an engine that takes stored energy from food and turns it into usable energy. That energy is used by your organs to maintain all of your bodily functions and to fuel your activities. This is how our bodies stay alive. Remove the energy from our bodies and you have a corpse. Since energy cannot be destroyed, where does it go?

As we exist in a three dimensional physical world, our understanding of energy is based in our reality. Energy is not just a property of the third dimension, it is a part of all other dimensions as well. At death, we leave the three dimensional physical world and return to the dimension of energy. As psychics or mediums, it is the energy dimension, or Spirit Plane, we are able to connect to and work with.

Your Personal Energy

Your spirit is made by the Creator and is infused with the divine spark of life. Your soul sits at the heart of your spirit and is the essence of your being. Just as a weakened heart will negatively affect your physical health, if your soul is empty, then your spirit energy is weakened as well.

Some believe that your spirit resides exclusively in your head or in your heart. This is incorrect. Your spirit is throughout your body. When your guides and masters wish to speak with you, they will utilize your spirit energy as the "phone cord" of communication. The stronger you can make your energy, the better connection you will have. Use love to fill your soul, as this will aid your energy in being stronger. Use meditation to help quiet your physical mind and body so when communication happens, there is less "static" on the line.

Personal Energy and Personality

Your unique personality will reflect how you work with your energy. Introverts by nature are quite reserved and hold their personal energy close to their physical bodies. Introverts in public situations will not push their energy out, but may hold it even closer to themselves like a protective blanket. In familiar surroundings, like home, introverts may actually open up their energy some so it extends out from the body a little bit more. Just because someone is holding their energy close, don't think they aren't using it to read people and situations.

Extroverts keep their energy at a distance from their physical bodies. These are people who, whether they know it or not, use their personal energy to "read" a room or people. Many extroverts are high energy people. This doesn't mean they're on the go all the time, it means they utilize their personal energy in an active fashion. Like a radar, a pulse goes out and they read the energy that comes back. This helps them interpret what is going on in a room and aids them in being their outgoing selves.

Food and Energy

In essence, your body is nothing more than an engine designed to carry your spirit around in the physical world. Like any engine, the purer the fuel you use to power it, the better the engine will run. This holds true when you are working as a psychic or a medium.

Having a diet that removes processed and junk foods will help your body maintain a higher energy level for you to work from. I'm not saying that an overweight, junk food eating psychic or medium is not a good one. I'm saying they have an added barrier to their abilities they could remove if they chose to do so.

Karma

Do unto others as you would have them do to you. Each of your actions creates a need for balance in the universe. A deed that is done in a positive way to another is paid back to you in a positive fashion. Likewise a negative deed is paid back negatively. This is the basis for karma.

It is believed that karma plays out not only in this lifetime but in other lifetimes as well. You cannot change your past actions. However, the choices you make in the present will affect your future. You can improve your future by making better choices and treating others honestly and with respect.

You can control what happens in your future. Start now to make it as good as it can be.

Thoughts Live

Your thoughts are energy. They have a life. Thoughts can be as loving or as angry as you make them. They are your thoughts, you own them. Thought is powerful. You can design your thoughts to help or hurt you or somebody else.

When you are working in the metaphysical world, you are working with energy. Your spiritual team will utilize energy to work with you. Their thoughts will be transferred to your thoughts by energy. Likewise, your thoughts are transferred to somebody else by energy.

Your thoughts set your intentions. If you think being psychic is phony and a joke, you will have difficulty learning and developing your abilities. You cannot read a book that is closed.

Opening your mind to accepting things you did not know and considering new thoughts and ideas will help you in developing your abilities. You are beginning a fascinating journey of self-discovery. Positive thoughts about yourself and what you are learning will determine how much you grow and how far your abilities develop.

Raising Your Energy the Love Way

In order to better work with your guides, masters, and angels, you will need to raise your energy vibration to make it easier for them to communicate with you. The more you are able to fill your soul with love, the stronger your energy will become.

What love level are you working out of? This is important because if you are working from one of the lower levels of love, you will not succeed in raising your energy. The more giving you are with your love, while maintaining proper ethical conduct with your energy, will help make your energy vibration higher. This in turn will make it easier for your guides, masters, and angels to communicate and work with you. This will also help you as you move further and develop as a medium.

Psychic and medium work is all about the energy. In order to move beyond the physical plane and reach those who are on the Spiritual Plane, a higher level of energy must be maintained by the psychic or medium. Increasing the energy you have to work with will aid you in becoming a better psychic or medium.

Levels of Love

I've broken down the concept of love into 5 categories as a base for looking at what types of energies you should be working with as a developing psychic.

Sex - *Primal & Raw* - This is a very selfish type of love, where the root of the emotion is based in pleasure or self-satisfaction. Some only view sex as love. When sex ends, so does their love. This is a very damaging type of love. In a solid, healthy relationship, sex is a wonderful sharing of the self and soul. Please do not confuse the difference in the two.

Respect - *Caring & Friendship* - This is a social type of love. It is the basis for how society functions. You do not want to hurt anyone, you act out of politeness (holding a door, saying please and thank you).

Compassion - *Emotional & Bonding* - This is a giving type of love. You provide or give without thought of being reimbursed. This type is normally what we consider "love" to be. It is the family love or marriage love.

Spiritual - *Parental & Sacrificing* - This is a love felt from our spirit or soul. This love gives of itself in every way, without thought of self, to any means including death. This is the love a parent has for a child. It is the love Christ exhibited from the cross.

God's Love - *Pure & Perfect* - This love is not understandable by physical man/woman. It is a love of complete understanding and forgiveness. We all carry the divine spark of life that comes from our Creator. We were created from this level of love.

As you develop and grow, you need to move toward a Compassion style love in your thoughts and actions. This brings a higher vibration in your energy which results in an easier connection to your guides and angels. It will also help you to keep a lid on your ego.

You will want to develop so you are working strictly from the Compassion and Spiritual levels of love outlined above. Work so that your thoughts match your actions. If you find yourself falling below these levels, know that your ego is trying to take control back.

Unconditional Love

Learn to develop unconditional love as you become more psychic. Love is the master of ego and will help you calm the excesses your ego creates. When you can work from a center of love, your psychic abilities open up and all connections become easier.

Unconditional love is what you should strive to achieve in both your personal and psychic lives. Having the ability to love all, regardless of what others have done to you, either real or perceived, will set yourself up for success. I do not mean you have to express unconditional love to everyone, especially after you have been wronged. Your ego bruises very easily. Do not allow ego pain to poison your well of love. You just need to acknowledge the situation and understand that other people are not perfect either. Use your love to forgive and allow yourself to move on. Forgiving and forgetting are two different concepts here, you can forgive with love but not forget what was done.

To act from ego means you are acting out of your lower, physical self or selfishness.

To act from love means you are acting out of your higher, spiritual self or selflessness.

A Good Ego

A level ego is what you must strive for, because a level ego will help protect you and keep you safe while connecting with your guides. It will also provide a very open and clear channel with your guides. It will help you recognize that working as a psychic or medium is about the people you are trying to help, not about yourself. A level ego will help you realize when you are getting too emotionally attached to a situation. It will also help you recognize when you have someone who is trying to emotionally dump on you or "vampire" your energy.

Should your ego start getting in the way, ground and center yourself so the connection to your guides becomes stronger. You will know when it wants attention because it will be causing doubt about information in your spiritual connection. It is always okay to take a few seconds to temper your ego and get rebalanced when needed.

Bad Ego, Bad

In psychic work, having a big ego means you will have big trouble. If you are having trouble with any area of your psychic work, I suggest you check out your ego first. When I started, my ego was **_HUGE!_** At the same time, I had a lot of trouble connecting to and hearing spirit. My ego was always second guessing things. You will never be able to fully remove your ego. Focus on reducing its impact on your thoughts and decisions. When you are able to limit your ego, your connection with your guides will flow. It is nice to go through the day having my guides drop in ideas and comments.

Your ego likes to show off. The "Hey, look at me" impulse is all ego. When you truly know your psychic gift is working, you will have a natural inclination to show it off. **DON'T!** That is ego talking, trying to take control back. Think of your ego as a 5-year-old child that wants your attention. When you focus your attention elsewhere, there is your ego trying to butt in.

Your ego is a deep canyon to spirit and spirit communication. Until you put ego in its place, you won't be able to bridge the gap. You must learn to trust what your guides are giving you. If your ego is not level, you're guides will not want to work with you. An out of balance ego works from a "woe is me" or "look at me" perspective.

Should you be looking at using your psychic or medium abilities to get rich or famous, that too is your ego at work. Focus first on developing your abilities. Use your talents to help others. When your abilities are strong and your work good, your guides will open doors for you. There have been many psychics and mediums who shot out of the gate with their ego leading the way. Their guides, realizing ego was in command, ended up leaving them high and dry.

Love's Unfortunate Counterpart

I challenge you to find one example in human history where an act of hate made everyone better. Don't get the act of hate confused with the acts of compassion and love that result from the original act of hate (terrorism, murder, bullying etc.). When an act of hate is unleashed, acts of love follow to balance it.

By learning to ground and center ourselves emotionally, we are better able to control our emotions. This calmness helps us to stand back from a situation and make the choice to work from a position of love. Where there is love, hate diminishes. When someone demonstrates love, we are all made better by it. Unfortunately, when someone demonstrates hate we are all affected as well, but not in a positive way.

Working or living out of hate will not allow your psychic abilities to bloom. Your guides, masters, and angels help you from a position of love. They will not help you enact hate. Use your love to control and eliminate hate from your life.

Hate is an emotion of the ego not getting its way. When you have this emotion, step back and examine it. Notice how it does not do you any good. Your spirit shrinks, your psychic energy is drained, and your ego gets larger. It becomes a vicious cycle with your spirit paying the price.

People may hate for any given reason; however, it generally stems from fear or ignorance. People fear things that are unfamiliar, different, or unusual. They also hate things they don't understand or that make them feel stupid. These traits may also be found in someone with a closed mind, who is either unable or unwilling to learn and discover new things.

A person's ego is a very fragile item. To challenge the ego or prove it wrong might lead to a wounded ego. Many feel a need to retaliate when their ego has been hurt and will lash out in unpleasant ways.

Controlling Hate

Hate gives another person power over you. When you hate people, you react to them in a negative way. Whether they are aware of it or not, you are giving them control. This is not a healthy dynamic for you. Again, step back and unemotionally recognize it for what it is. Once it is recognized, you can learn, accept, release, and then grow.

When working as a psychic or medium, you should be working to help clients, not harm them. If your readings are not based out of love and caring, you are not well suited for psychic work. If you do not work from love, then you are working from something less than love. This is where the ego steps in, apathy develops, and soon a mild hatred takes root. Do not be one of these people. Always give love and always give energy. This is the way of an honest lightworker.

Making Energy Psychic

We are energy beings having a physical experience. The sooner you not only understand but also accept it, the easier time you will have developing as a psychic or medium.

Energy is the heart of being a psychic or medium. Everything you do will have a connection to energy. Generally, psychics connect to the energy of the living, whereas mediums connect to the energy of the living *and* those in spirit. This doesn't mean that as a normal person you will not be able to connect with your guides, masters, and angels if you are not a medium. Actually, your guides, masters, and angels have been doing the heavy lifting of contact with you up to now. They have had to use their energy to connect with you. Now, you are using your energy to connect with them. Because of your new focus with your energy, your relationship with them will blossom. Messages from them will become clearer and you will feel their presence around you more often.

When doing a reading, connect your energy to that of the person for whom you are reading. When working on contacting those in spirit, raise your energy up to help make the connection stronger. Use your psychic self-defense tools to keep your energy safe while working. This will not block your ability to connect, but will keep you protected.

When needing to connect to another for a reading, imagine taking a blanket and tossing it over you and your client. Both of you are now in the same energy space. Should you be doing a reading over a long distance, you can send out a long tendril to connect with them. One of the easiest methods I have discovered is to connect right through the phone. Your phone is next to your head, their phone is next to theirs, just connect like they are right next to you.

Empaths have a natural ability to connect with and understand energy. These people feel the energy of others and are able to pick up emotional changes that occur. Unfortunately, this also means that they will take on the energy or emotion of another without realizing it. Empaths will want to develop a strong psychic self-defense practice.

Ethics and Energy

Make sure as you do your energy work it is done in an honest and ethical manner. When using energy with people, follow this simple guideline: **You are not allowed to use your energy to read people without their permission.**

You wouldn't want me connecting my energy to you and using it to learn private information about you then sharing it publicly, the same goes for you. If you are doing a psychic reading, only connect to the person you are reading. Performing readings on a third person is not ethical. Let me be very direct here. When you do a reading, other people around your client may appear, and that is okay. However, if a client wants you to do a reading on someone else and provide the information to them, that is where the ethical line is crossed. If you feel you are being asked to do something unethical, protect your energy and your karma and politely refuse.

As a medium, you have the ability to connect energetically to those who have died. It is just as unethical to interrupt someone on the Spiritual Plane as well. If they want to come through to the person you are working with, fine; if not, let it be. Likewise, creating a chain of people and using your energy to connect to the fifth person in that chain is not ethical. Just because you _can_ does not mean you _should_.

"Who's gonna stop me if I use energy this way," has probably crossed your mind. That is your ego talking, and we know when it talks, it's not good for you or your psychic development. First, your guides, masters, and angels will back away from helping you. Your ego will fill in the void they leave behind and a world of trouble will ensue. Second, karma will bring about its balance, and whatever damage you have caused will be visited upon you. Lastly, those you have hurt will know you are not trustworthy.

Should you start doing readings for people, the information you obtain during those readings stays in those readings. **What you see here, say here, feel here, and hear here, stays here when you leave here** is a great mantra. If a client gives you permission to discuss their reading with someone else, then ethically you are fine to do so.

If a client wants you to reach out into another person's energy, this is a no-no too. You can provide information that relates to the client regarding another person, but to read someone else and give that personal information to a client is ethically wrong.

Honesty, integrity, and the highest ethics are needed to function as a skilled psychic or medium. Anything less and you are inviting trouble.

Because the job of a psychic or medium is not very well understood by the population at large, our skill is often perceived to be fraudulent or a scam. Should you work to reinforce this stereotype you will be doing yourself and countless others a disservice.

Working with ethics when using your energy will open doors for you. Clients want the help of an honest and ethical psychic or medium. Your guides, masters, and angels will develop a stronger connection to you, making your work easier.

In the end, the choice is yours. Karma is as karma does.

Energy Vampires

In my time reading, I have run into energy vampires. They exist not only as clients, but also as readers. These people enjoy sucking the energy right out of you the way a vampire sucks blood. I tend to see this in people who are always the victim in all situations. I'm not saying their problems aren't real, it's just that in life, we can choose not to be the victim.

We have all encountered the person who if it wasn't for bad luck they would have no luck at all. These "woe is me" people then get sympathy from others. That is a form of energy exchange. The ego and energy of the vampire is boosted by the sympathizer. As a result, the ego enjoys the power and seeks to do it again. It's kind of like a drug for the vampire. Many don't realize they're doing it, but that doesn't make it right. Refuse to allow your energy to be taken by a vampire by making sure you use your psychic energy protection tools.

Forgiveness Is NOT About Them

Hate, anger, rage, jealousy, etc., are all based in the negative. They diminish your personal energy. This does nothing to aid in your spiritual growth. Hate, anger, jealousy, etc., are all based in the ego. Allowing the ego to control you makes your spiritual energy smaller and your light becomes dimmer. Your guides and angels are less interested in working with someone who is based in the ego.

Forgiveness helps you release negativity and grow beyond a situation. That doesn't mean you're going to be best friends with the person who wronged you. It means that you have recognized the situation, learned from it, accepted it, and then released it. Remember, you are here to learn and grow, and forgiveness provides exactly that.

The process of forgiveness also helps you work from a higher love level. By releasing your negative emotions, your personal energy increases and you become a brighter light. Your guides and angels have an easier time working with someone who has higher energy and a clearer light.

Whatever the situation, each person will have his or her own karma to deal with and work through. Having a conscious understanding of cause and effect will help you to have a healthier karmic balance.

While forgiving others is beneficial, do not forget to forgive yourself. We are often hardest on ourselves and do not show ourselves the love of forgiveness. Each of us is human and making mistakes is part of that. Everyone wishes they could go back in time and say or do something different. Accepting that events unfold in a particular way and that it is part of the universal design may help your mind come to terms with something. Forgiveness is there to heal your heart and bring peace.

Reason, Season, Lifetime

Because we are here to learn and grow not just as people, but as spiritual beings, we need to understand that not all things are meant for us.

Some people are with us only for a reason. To teach us, guide us, or enact karmic balance. Others will be with us for a season in our lives. This might be for a few weeks, few months, few years, or even a few decades. There will be some who will be with us for most of our lifetime.

Emotionally, it can be very hard to let go of someone, especially when love is involved. Understanding that either we or they have served the intended purpose and it is time to move on is difficult. Stagnation and discord are often signs of when a relationship has run its course.

When one party changes and the other does not accept or follow that change, it is time to let them go so everyone can continue to grow. To continue to hold on to someone out of fear or selfishness keeps everyone from discovering, learning, and growing as we are intended to do.

God and Religion

It is impossible to be a practicing psychic and not have a belief in God.

Now, let me clarify a little. There are many different names for God that are used around the world. By the term "God," I am merely referencing the spiritual being who created everything. Although your name for him/her may be different from mine, your belief in a God is what is important.

Without a belief in God, you cannot grow psychically. Working as a psychic or medium means you are working with energy of the Spiritual Plane. You are actually able to communicate with that energy. Your experience in communicating with spirits, guides, and angels helps prove that God exists and is part of every human being.

Psychics, Mediums, and Modern Religion

As I do my psychic work, I remain comforted by 1 Corinthians 14:1 "Follow the way of love and eagerly desire spiritual gifts, especially the gift of prophecy." (Holy Bible, New International Version)

I find it interesting that the clergy would judge all psychics and mediums as frauds, while they are teaching from a book written, in part, by psychics and mediums. Many parts of the Bible are written by prophets who foretold of future events (psychics) while others spoke with angels or those who had died (mediums).

Many religions regard psychics and mediums as nothing more than charlatans and con artists. Unfortunately, there are psychics and mediums out there who give credence to that. Do not be one of those! Rather, allow your work as a psychic or medium to always be exceptionally honest and of the highest ethical standards. Doing this will help raise your energy vibration and assist with your development.

As a psychic or medium you will discover that well-intentioned people will try to save you from this "evil." You will not be able to change their minds about how you work with spirit or about how this is not evil. Be respectful to them and always act from love when explaining your position. If their debate with you draws a crowd, your attitude of love toward the other person will be remembered. If you act out of ego, your words and actions will never be forgotten.

Following the way of love as you do this will help bring you to a higher vibration. Not only will others on the earthly plane of existence be drawn to you, but so will your guides, masters, and angels. This will also help draw you closer and find favor in the eyes of our Creator.

Our Spiritual Team

We all have guides, masters, and angels helping us in our lives. Have you suddenly had the answer to a vexing problem just drop into your head? Have you ever had a thought about doing or not doing something only to find out later that had you acted, you would have been harmed? These are examples of our guides, masters, and angels at work in our lives.

My guides are with me all the time and I welcome their input whenever they want to give it. They have provided insight which has aided me with my problems, and I consistently ask for and thank them for their help. There have been times writing this book where I've struggled with my ideas. When this happens, I pause for a moment to ground and center myself. I ask for insight so I can continue writing, and a word or phrase will come to me to get me going again.

If you do not believe in your guides, masters, and angels, they will still be there for you. However, your lack of belief will make it harder for them to communicate and for you to receive their messages. I can tell you it is amazing to have a relationship with them as they are helpful, informative, and quite fun to have with you.

Guides and Masters

Before we are born, we make arrangements on the Spirit Plane with those who will be our guides and masters. Some are with us for our whole lifetime, while others come and go as situations require. The important thing to know is that they are always there for us.

Guides and masters are there to help with our problems, but they are not there to take care of our problems. We must do the work, the heavy lifting, to resolve our issues. They are our teachers and will guide us to grow, but they will not do the work for us.

Guides and masters appreciate being recognized for helping you. It's not like you have to bake them a chocolate cake. Telling them "Thank you" and being appreciative of them is positive energy and that is the reward they like.

There will be times where they are silent watchers of your life. This is a "test" phase as you learn a new lesson or grow your spirit. There will also be times where their absence will be felt because you are going against their advice.

Guides and Masters – Communication

In order for your guides and masters to communicate with you, you need to raise your spiritual energy level and they need to lower theirs. Your guides and masters will utilize many different ways to communicate with you. Generally, they will work with the system you set up for them. However, do not be surprised if they end up using some of your "clair" abilities.

One of the ways guides and masters communicate is through thought. When I get information from my guides it feels like it is spoken directly in the center of my brain. I will suddenly have a new idea in my head that I had not had before. My favorite is when they drop in funny information about things. My guides have a killer sense of humor and I love having them with me.

Guides and masters can also communicate in a physical form. This is done in a variety of ways. For example, you can arrange with your guides to "show" you an image or item when they are trying to communicate with you. Let's say your image is a camel. Then during the course of a day or two, you might encounter a few images of camels, find a show on television with a camel in it, see an empty box of Camel cigarettes, and have someone talk to you about camels. This is when you need to pay attention to your thoughts or what is happening around you because it has significance.

Another way they communicate physically is with words. Like in the above example where someone talks to you about camels, your guides and masters will put people around you who will say, almost verbatim, what your guides and masters want you to hear. It may happen multiple times to help you get the message.

Guides and masters may also use your sense of feel, smell, or taste to alert you to things. How many times have you had a bad feeling about something and did not do it only to be proven right? Trust these communications when they happen.

If you feel they just sent you a message and you didn't quite get it, ask them to send it again. They are there to help and will resend the information. The bridge between our slower physical-based spiritual energy and their pure spiritual energy is what causes the confusion sometimes. Keeping yourself grounded and centered will help make this connection easier.

Angels

There are some similarities and differences between angels and guides and masters. Angels will communicate with you like your guides and masters do. Angels are also there to help you out when you are in need.

Because the energy of angels is very pure and very strong, they have more of an ability to interact on the physical plane than guides or masters do. Their knowledge is also greater than that of a guide or master. Guides and masters get the big picture, angels get the whole picture. Angels also differ from guides and masters in another important way. Angels have never incarnated as a human, whereas guides and masters have.

Asking angels for assistance is the best way to bring them around. They are there to serve us, but they are not there to do for us. Asking for angelic assistance all the time will tire them of you. Make sure you are at a point where you need assistance, not where you're too lazy to do the work yourself.

Like guides and masters, always thank angels for their assistance.

Levels on the Spiritual Plane

The Spiritual Plane is where we come from and where we will return. While we can learn and grow on the Spiritual Plane, our advancement happens faster when we learn on the physical plane. When we return to the Spiritual Plane we still have the ability to communicate, observe, and visit those on the physical plane.

The exact number of levels on the Spiritual Plane is not clear. What is clear is that as spirits we yearn to exist on higher levels. We wish to advance as spiritual beings, which brings us closer to our Creator.

When we reach a certain level of development, we no longer have to come to the physical plane to learn. Instead, we work to help others who are on the physical plane. Some may become guides and teachers for those working to better themselves. Others will work at improving themselves on the Spiritual Plane.

Spirits vs. Ghosts vs. Entities

Spirits are those who have died, left their physical form, and crossed into the light, returning to the Spiritual Plane. Ghosts are those who have died and chosen to remain on our physical plane. Entities are those who may or may not have previously existed on the physical plane. They exist as the lowest of the levels of energy and work to possess or control the living. It is not easy to differentiate between the three. Generally, a spirit who has crossed into the light will act and work with you in a loving way. A ghost will act and work in a selfish way. An entity will act and work in a way to possess or control you. As a psychic or medium, you will need to learn to discern between the differing energies of spirits, ghosts, entities, and those of your guides, masters, and angels.

When doing readings for clients it is important to be grounded and protected. When connecting to the Spirit Plane, ghosts or entities might try to attach themselves to you. You will want to learn how to discern between the lower energy of ghosts or entities and the higher energy of spirit. Will you be bringing in the sweet, loving grandmother who has crossed or will you be bringing in the mean, abusive, alcoholic uncle who didn't cross? Which one would you like to have connecting to your energy? Always use your protection when doing readings for others.

Spirits from the light will exit after the session has ended. They will not try to influence you later. They will leave when asked. They have other things to do than to stay with you on the physical plane.

Ghosts will attempt to stick with you once a session has ended. They will start their relationship with you by acting like your best friend, helping you where they can. This will turn ugly when they start to control you and give you bad information. They will try to stroke your ego and make you reliant on them. They will not go away when asked.

Entities are about control. They will work to gain your confidence much the way a ghost would. Once you allow an entity in, they will push you aside and will control your thoughts and actions. Removing them is very difficult and may require an exorcism.

Don't think this could not happen to you. They are out there and unfortunately, they are real. Should you encounter this situation, you need to use your psychic protection to help break the attachment the ghost or entity has created. Call in assistance from your guides, masters, and angels as well.

Lower Entities

As a beginning psychic, your unfamiliarity with spirits on the other side can present a danger to you. Just because something is in spirit form does not mean it is enlightened or is there to help you. Lower entities may try to pose as guides, loved ones, angels, or other ascended beings. Existing on the Spirit Plane allows them to move without the restraint of time. Therefore, lower entities will have access to information just like your guides or angels. It is how they use and manipulate this information that sets them apart.

At first, they will provide you with accurate information, to gain your trust. As time progresses, their information becomes very inaccurate. They will start to tell you lies and try to get you to do things that you normally would not do. Using Ouija boards is a notorious way to attract a lower entity to you.

Early on you should try to meet your guides, masters, and angels who work to help you. Get a sense of their energy so you know when they are around. Ask them to protect you and only allow evolved spirits that are there for a higher purpose to come into contact with you.

Possessions

Possession is very real and should be avoided. An enlightened spirit, angel, or guide will never try to possess you without your permission. While not all earthbound ghosts may attempt to possess or harm you, there are some that will. There are lower entities that may try to possess you as well. Should a ghost or entity make their presence known to you and attempt to possess you, use your psychic defense immediately and DO NOT ALLOW THEM IN. Also be aware that they may try to claim they are of the highest angelic realms as part of their deception. Do not fall for any of this. It's a good idea to always practice your psychic protection and grounding exercises.

There are some very skilled mediums who are able to do trance work or channeling. This allows the spirit to share the body, yet allows the medium some control over the process. Please do not attempt this until you have years of experience and are able to distinguish between high vibration spirits, masters, and angels and those that are not. Make sure your guides are present to help you stay in control of the experience. Even when just starting out, it would be wise to have someone there to provide a physical presence, just in case.

Psychic and Medium

These two words are often misunderstood to mean the same thing, yet they are different. Below are my definitions of these two abilities and how they differ. Many want you to think that both do the same thing. They do not. As you move through this book I feel it is important to draw a distinction between the two abilities.

Psychic – A person who has sensitivity to nonphysical or supernatural forces. This person may have a hypersensitivity to energy or the way energy relates to them. They are able to interpret information utilizing one or more of their "clair" senses.

Medium – A person who possesses psychic abilities but also has the added ability of being able to interact and communicate with those who exist on the Spiritual Plane.

A medium is always psychic, while a psychic is not always a medium.

Abilities and Time

We all have a very basic level of psychic ability. You have probably already noticed that you have one ability that is stronger than the others. Clairvoyance, clairaudience, clairsentience, clairgustance, and clairalience are the five psychic senses you can use to obtain spiritual information. Your goal is to work with your strongest sense while developing your other abilities over time.

When I started, I was predominantly clairsentient. My clairvoyant and clairaudient abilities were slim to none. Time and work have helped me to develop my other "clairs." I am now quite attuned at hearing spirit (clairaudience) and seeing the images (clairvoyance) they wish to present to me.

This is not an overnight process. It will take months, if not years, to fully master. Remember, your thoughts set your intentions. Meditation, exercises, finding a development circle, reading, and learning more about psychic abilities will aid in this process. Your guides, masters, and angels will assist you with your growth when they know you are serious.

How Psychic Information Works – Not the Whole Movie

In 30 seconds, the TV ad has to make you interested in a 2-hour movie. They show you 10 fast sequenced scenes of high action and drama in hopes it will convince you that the remaining 1 hour and 59 minutes are just as good. Welcome to a psychic reading. Skeptics think you have the whole movie, director notes, photographs, interviews with the actors, and everything is in 3-D!!

When you are giving a psychic reading, you will get bits of information, kind of like the TV ad. You will need to ask questions to clarify your information, to get the whole picture. Don't ask leading questions, ask clarifying ones instead.

Consider this: Everyone has grandparents, so if you say to a client, "who's the old guy," that's fishing for information, that's not psychic. However, if you say, "I see an older gentleman in bib overalls with a fishing pole and a red baseball hat, do you recognize this person?" that is specific, that is psychic. Now you have to figure out why that person has shown up, what is his message, what is the importance? Sure, grandpa may just want to say "hi" or let you know he was there for a family birthday party last week. But you will not always get all of that. Asking questions of a client that will clarify information, not provide you information, is how to work. The difference is looking like an honest psychic or a fraud.

Do not expect to get every aspect of a reading correct either. The connection between spirit and the psychic/medium does not allow for all knowledge about everything. There will be times when you will get information that is extremely accurate. There will be times you may only get a sense or feeling about something. The whole movie will never come into focus. Trust the scenes you receive because these are the ones that your client needs to know about.

Use Your Guides to Protect You

As a psychic or medium reader you will come to understand that not all spirits are good, which is why practicing psychic protection is important. If any information you receive is negative, you will know it is not from a spirit, guide, master, or angel. By negative I don't mean bad news, I mean information that makes you act in a negative way.

As a medium, you will be in contact with spirits who have passed and are sending love back to the physical plane. Work with your guides, masters, and angels to assist you to be in contact with only those spirits who are acting out of love.

You can tell your guides how you want them to work to keep the lower, negative ghost or entity energy away from you. It doesn't have to be anything difficult or fancy, it just needs to be established for your protection. Your guides are there to help you and will protect you as well.

Be The Conduit,
Not The Conductor

When giving readings, remember, you are the speaker for spirit, providing information. It is up to the client to determine what to do with the information. If the client does not act upon what you have given, that is up to them, not you.

It is difficult to give a reading that includes something negative. It is not our place to make a change that is not ours to make. Being confident in our abilities is one thing, but trying to make someone change themselves based on a reading we give is wrong. Please provide what spirit gives and then let it go.

Psychic Hippocratic Oath

The Hippocratic Oath was written by Hippocrates thousands of years ago. It is an oath that many physicians consider sacred to their practice of medicine. Included in the oath is the responsibility to treat the patient with utmost care, protect the privacy of the patient, and to teach the secrets of medicine. Basically, the physician is promising not to do harm to their patient.

It is my belief that psychics and mediums should consider this oath as a guideline to working with their clients. People will come to you with concerns and troubles. They are unsure about what the future may hold and are seeking your insight. Treating them with care should be a goal for all psychics and mediums.

While giving readings, there will be times you will receive bad or negative information for the sitter. How you deliver that information can be as gentle as a feather or as hard as a brick. Regrettably, there are psychics who hit clients with the brick, and as a result, act in a way that is not in their clients' best interests. Let us consider two situations:

An elderly client comes in for a reading. During that reading you get a strong feeling of the client's passing. You can say to the client, "I see you're going to be dying soon," or "I see you are preparing for a most amazing journey."

A client comes in concerned about his work situation. You sense that he is about to lose his job. You can say to the client, "You are going to be fired," or "You will have new career opportunities coming your way."

Using softer phrases doesn't make your information incorrect. Remember, the clients are aware of their situations as well. Clients will also interpret your words in the way they want. As a psychic or medium your words carry heavy weight and can influence clients much more than you are aware. Always complete the reading on a positive note. Leave clients feeling good about themselves or their situations.

Public Psychic/Medium

You've worked hard, developed your abilities, and decided you would like to start doing readings professionally. First, let me say that it is your decision as to when you are ready for this. Your guides will help you with timing by presenting you with opportunities. Should you jump in too early, you will find yourself struggling. Your desire to read for the public should not be based on your ego, but on your ability to connect to your guides and using your skills to help people.

Second, here are a few tips as you prepare to enter the public arena. Announcing you are psychic means friends, relatives, and acquaintances may ridicule you. You will need to have or develop a thick skin. Some will laugh at you in front of you, others only behind your back. This journey **will** change you. You will need to learn to let go of relationships that no longer work for your highest good.

Third, be prepared to be attacked. These attacks are not physical but personal. They are based in the opinions of those making the allegations. Because the world of the psychic/medium is misunderstood by so many, you will encounter people who feel they must challenge or ridicule you. The public likes nothing more than tearing someone down, especially psychics. They seem to think psychics and mediums know everything and see everything and when something is wrong or something doesn't happen the way you say it will, you are a fraud. There is nothing you can say or do to change their minds. Save yourself the trouble and avoid arguing with them.

There are also many positives for taking on this work. You are on an enlightening adventure of self-discovery, self-improvement, and personal growth. It will be never ending. The work you do can be very rewarding, and I don't mean just financially. Sure, it's nice to be paid, but you will discover that giving good readings will be its own reward. You are a trusted source of information for people who are letting you into their energy and secrets. You must maintain the highest ethics, protecting the confidence clients have put in you. You will also meet many wonderful people who share your interests and beliefs.

Just because you discover you have a psychic gift, doesn't mean you have to go public. It is fine to use your ability for your own purposes or with your family and friends.

First Reading

After learning to read tarot, I wanted to practice with my friends and obtain validations on my readings. One of my first readings was with my teacher, Sylvia. When I arrived, we sat down at a table and chatted for a few minutes. As I got my cards out to start the reading, I stopped for a second and asked her if her husband was going to be changing jobs. Sylvia stopped cold and told me that her husband had just gotten an offer on a job that he had long sought. She also told me that they had told nobody yet about the change. Although the formal tarot reading had not started yet, this is a good example to show you to pay attention to information before a reading. She was both astounded and amazed that I would get that information. Her validation was a huge boost to my knowing I was on the right track.

It felt really good to get information before the reading actually started. It taught me to trust information when it comes in, regardless of timing.

The Psychic/Medium Business

Once you decide to read for the public, you need to consider the business side of being psychic. You will be accepting money for your time and talent. Set a price for what you think is fair and do not let others tell you what to charge. If you decide on a price that is too low, people may not take you seriously or you will find yourself overwhelmed with readings. That could cause you to stop enjoying your gift and start to hate it. A rate that is too high, especially for someone just starting out, can hurt you before you develop a client base. Charge one rate across the board. Your time and talent has value.

Do you need to rent space? Will you be reading at psychic fairs? Will you be working out of your home? Are there travel costs? You need to charge enough to cover your expenses and time.

You also might consider advertising. Word of mouth has always been a great way to build a personal services business. You will need to give thought about how you desire to promote yourself. Putting advertisements in newspapers can get expensive, fast. Starting out, find ways to advertise by spending as little as you can. Use social media to connect with friends and clients. Ask a local new age store if you can put flyers in their store or fill in as a psychic reader. Contact a local radio station to do readings for the host or for listeners. Find out if there are any new age fairs or paranormal events in your area.

Websites are a great way to help you bring in business. You do not have to be a web designer to build one. There are many web hosting companies that allow you to build your own site. It can be as simple as one page or more complex, with multiple pages. Naming the site is up to you. Make sure your web address is something the client can remember. Your name can also be a powerful tool. I utilize mine with my website, cbbjork.com.

When you create business cards or flyers, make them professional. These items represent and promote you. Many business cards allow for both sides to be printed. Utilize this to get your message out. Don't just do a card with your name, the title of "psychic" and your phone number. Provide your business email address, your web address, and your Facebook page. If you are regularly on other social media platforms and wish to promote yourself that way, add those as well. Remember to list all of the services you offer.

On anything you use to promote yourself, make sure to proofread it before publishing it. Your goal is to always promote yourself in a positive and professional manner.

Power of Your Name

When starting to read professionally, I was concerned about keeping my personal life separate from my psychic endeavors. I was thinking about coming up with some sort of "business name" that I would work under. I inquired with different psychics about why they chose to work under a given title or name. The information I received was helpful.

A good friend of mine advised me to use my personal name and not to use a fancy business name. She told me, "Your name is your most powerful tool for doing this work and will help in building your professional reputation." She advised me to do all my marketing around my name.

I have found her advice to be very sound. Should you decide to become a professional psychic, your name can be one of your strongest assets. There is a lot of energy around your name, which is why it can be positive.

Your Ego and Readings

When you are giving readings, do not allow your ego to get in the way. Your ego will try to tell you what you are getting is wrong. It will try to stop you from providing the information your guides are giving. The information you receive will sometimes be confusing, and it may not make sense. Remember, you are there to relay the message, spirit provides the message. Your ego does not like being ignored, so it tries to interfere with the message by putting its own interpretation on the information. No matter how weird or bizarre the message, deliver the information. It will make sense to the client once you speak it into life.

Sober Psychic/Medium

When you are working as a psychic or medium, using any type of alcohol or drugs is a *MAJOR NO-NO!!* If you enjoy that type of lifestyle, this is not the work for you. Anyone who is a recreational user of alcohol and/or drugs is not able to be a clear channel for spirit, guides, masters, or angels to use. On top of that, there are lower level entities and ghosts who may form an attachment to those who have an addiction.

I'm not saying you can't go out and have a beer or a glass of wine with dinner. Once you introduce alcohol into your system though, you are done being a psychic or medium for that day.

Some believe that using recreational drugs opens their mind or helps them connect. I'm sorry, but that is ego talking. If you enjoy recreational drug use, please do not make it part of your psychic or medium practice.

Daily prescription medications do not fall into this category. If you are taking any medications that make you feel off or unable to connect, refrain from your psychic endeavors until you are fully recovered.

The Fuzzy Client

When doing psychic or medium readings for clients, you will undoubtedly encounter the "Fuzzy Client." This doesn't mean someone who forgot to shave, but instead refers to their energy. When doing the reading, you will have a hard time connecting to their energy. It is almost like it is moving about, making it difficult to establish a firm connection.

The reason for this may be that your client is feeling the effects of alcohol or recreational drugs. Just like it is difficult for the psychic/medium to use their energy for a reading after being intoxicated, it is so for the client as well.

When this person comes for a reading, you will work to connect and have a hard time getting solid information. It is easy for your frustration to grow in this instance, which will hinder your reading. Should this happen, do not assume it is because of you. Anytime you encounter this, stop the reading and inform the client you are having some difficulty connecting. You don't have to accuse them of intoxication. Just let them know that there are certain things that prevent you from making a solid connection for a reading, like when a client is closed off or has been recently intoxicated. If you can't get past the fuzziness, it's okay to stop the reading and not charge them.

It takes a lot of energy from the psychic/medium to work with this client and can drain your energy. In some respects it's like encountering a psychic vampire. If you are doing a group of readings together, this client can leave you drained and less effective for the ones to follow. Take a short break and recharge yourself by grounding and then performing psychic self-defense.

When I do tarot parties, I ask the clients not to drink before their readings, as that would hinder my effectiveness and keep them from enjoying their readings.

Taking Your Energy on the Road

The most important skill to develop as a psychic or medium is the ability to use energy. It is important to almost all aspects of your work. The more you develop your energy, the more you will discover the fascinating things that can be done with it. It does not matter what your clair gift is, all of them benefit from energy.

You will discover you can take your energy and connect to another person's energy. This skill will help you do better readings. By connecting to their energy, you will discover a new depth to your readings.

It does not have to stop there. Animals and environments have their own energy fields as well. You can explore jungles or oceans by tapping into their energy. Why stop there, because the whole galaxy is full of energy bodies you can reach out to.

Psychics, Mediums, and Ghosts

If you are developing as a psychic or a medium, you will need to get used to encountering ghosts. Your development means you will have a higher energy vibration, which in turn attracts ghosts to you. While the specific psychic or medium work you do may not directly put you into contact with them, your need to be aware of them is important.

Practice psychic protection before you open yourself up to do psychic or medium work. Learn to communicate with your guides so they do not allow ghosts to interfere when working with the Spiritual Plane. In time you will learn to tell the difference between ghost, spirit, and angel energy and how to recognize when they are around.

Spirit Speak

Whether it is a guide, master, angel, or spirit who has crossed over, there are times you will be confused by the information they provide. Information from spirit is not always picture perfect. The best way to interpret messages is to be as simple as possible. Give exactly what you are getting, no matter how strange. This is when you have to trust it through. Consider these examples of when I used my own interpretation instead of what was provided and how that steered the reading off course:

Clairvoyance: During a reading about a gentleman who had passed, I clearly saw the man being torn in two. I had already determined he died from a heart condition, so this was not about his death. I interpreted it as he had two personalities. This was not received well by my client. Confused, I told the sitter what I saw and was advised that being torn in two made perfect sense. The gentleman's children lived in two separate areas, one in Indiana and the other in Texas, and he was torn between the two.

Clairaudience: A client came to me for a tarot reading about her work situation. She was seeking some clarity about what was to come. During the reading I sensed my guides providing information about her supervisor. When I asked what was important about the relationship between the two, I clearly heard the word "wimp." I told the client her supervisor was a wimp who was afraid to help her succeed. The reading became a little jumbled and confused. Again, I mentioned to the client that when I asked my guides about their relationship I heard "wimp." I assumed it was directed at the supervisor. The client told me how she was intimidated by her supervisor and that applied more to her. This revelation changed the end of the reading and gave the client a great outcome.

In both of these situations, what spirit provided was spot on, but my attempts to interpret made them spot off. As a psychic or medium, spirit holds the microphone and we are the speaker that the client hears. If we try to put our own values or interpretations on what spirit is communicating, the message gets garbled. Spirit actually tries working with us as simply as possible. Being simple in your delivery will be appreciated on both sides.

Encountering Mom in Spirit

"Remember the Sabbath to keep it Holy," was the initial statement made by one of my classmates as we were working with a tipping table. "That sounds like my mother," I quickly responded. It had been more than a year since she had died and about a year since I had helped her cross over. I had hoped she would come through. I was thrilled she decided to stop in.

A tipping table is a form of physical mediumship where a spirit can use the energy of the people around the table and cause it to tip. You ask a question and invite the spirit to respond by tipping the table in a certain direction. This is a time-tested and easy way to make contact with those on the other side. The four of us in my group sit on opposite sides of the table, allowing it to tip to whomever it desires to communicate with.

My mom was able to verify that she had made it into the light and was doing fine on the other side. She sent her love to me and my sisters and was very happy to be reunited with many of her family members. It was a wonderful session, she was very communicative and moved the table with ease.

As the session came to a close, I asked her, "Do you have any last messages for me?" The table literally wobbled over to me and then tipped itself into my lap like it was giving me a hug. I responded by hugging the table and telling my mother she can come through any time she desires. What a wonderful way to end the session!!

Difficulty in the Reading

When you start reading for clients you will discover some people are very open and easy to read and others are not. This happens to everyone who does this work. Learning how to work through it and not taking it personally are important.

Some clients will sit down with almost a "prove it" attitude. I've never understood this mindset. Why go to a psychic if you don't believe in the first place? This attitude is difficult to overcome because getting them to open up does not always work.

Other clients are open but will not realize they are closed off to your reading. These types are easier to work with. To remedy this situation, just pause the reading for a moment. Advise the client you are having some difficulty connecting and ask them if they would take a deep breath and exhale. If needed, you can ask them as they exhale to also let their guard down a little too. Usually the deep breath helps calm their anxiety/stress/block and gives you an opening to make a better connection.

Another way to make a solid connection is to have some of their energy. You can do this by holding their hand or something that is strongly connected to their energy. A set of car keys or jewelry usually works. These items have been in their possession and have absorbed your clients energy. Remember to give back whatever you have borrowed from the client. This type of reading can be stronger because you are using psychometry in addition to how you normally read.

If all attempts to open the client fails, do not be afraid to end the reading. It is better to tell the client that you are just having a bad day and can't give them the reading they deserve than to flub through it hoping to get something. I don't charge a client when this happens. I feel it is up to me to connect and if I can't do it, they don't owe me. My reputation is more important to me than money.

Dealing with Death

Death will make its appearance in your readings if you do this long enough. This is probably the hardest topic to discuss with a client. When a death becomes apparent in your reading, do not shy away from it, but be gentle. People come to a psychic looking for hope. In general, most people fear death, whether it's their own or someone else's. I'm not saying to give them false hope, which would be wrong. Instead, use gentle words. Don't say "death," "die," or "dead." Use neutral words that don't have such a negative feel. "Passing," "crossing," or "at peace" all have a gentler impact.

Please understand that your words in a death reading are more important than in any other reading you will do. The effect of what you say may be very distressing to the client. Do not let them leave your reading on a negative note. Do what you can to comfort them and give them something positive and uplifting to end the reading.

The Hardest Reading - Yourself

Should you decide to work on doing readings for yourself and others, you will likely encounter a common problem. Many people who do readings for themselves have a hard time getting the information correct due to personal bias. Generally, our thoughts about ourselves are not grounded in reality. Our self-perception is either too negative or too positive. This translates into trouble reading ourselves because we take this unrealistically negative or positive view into the reading. Should you notice this, you might wish to seek readings from another psychic or medium.

Reading for close friends or family can prove tricky as well. When you are emotionally attached to someone, you may have difficulty giving negative or hard information as part of the reading.

I believe this is because of our familiarity with their energy. People we are connected to and share an ongoing bond with can be harder to read. It is difficult to give negative information to those we care about. In response, we unconsciously try to make them happy and only discuss the good in the reading. This causes us to get the information wrong.

Another aspect of reading those close to you is that they can be more afraid about what you learn than what you do not. Everyone has secrets. Be they thoughts, emotions, or actions, these private things can terrify people if others discover them. This may lead those close to you being harder to read than a stranger.

Should you wish to read for those closest to you, let them know in advance you will provide the good, bad, and ugly of the reading. Let them decide if they still want you to do the reading. Working as the honest psychic or medium that you are will help to boost your confidence and abilities.

Psychic and Forget It

It doesn't matter for whom you are reading, give the reading and forget it. Your role in the psychic reading is to act as a conduit for spirit. Do not judge your clients or their situations. Do not discuss readings with others under any circumstances. Whatever information you obtain during a reading is only for the person sitting with you. If they decide to share the information, that is their choice, not yours.

The 100% Psychic

As a psychic, you will never be 100% right on all things. With work you may reach 80-90% accuracy, which is impressive. Any psychic that claims an accuracy of 100% is not being honest. These psychics are working from their ego. Be honest as you do your work. Most people who come to a psychic for a reading do not expect 100% accuracy.

Darksiders

There are "psychic readers" out there who work from a level of low energy and ego. This is dangerous to the public. These are the readers who manipulate clients, cast curses, blackmail, etc. If you encounter one of these, **RUN!!!**

So, how are they "psychic"? They learned and developed the ability naturally, but at some point their ego and/or lower entities got the better of them. Lower entities will provide accurate information to the psychic to gain your trust. Additionally, it is possible for a negative psychic to connect into your energy field and read you. This is why initially their info might be good but once they try to push deeper, their abilities and information weaken and they resort to unethical practices.

True psychics and mediums do nothing of the sort. They work from a base of love and seek out only those energies that exist for a higher good. Honest psychics and mediums will charge a reasonable fixed fee for their services and will never try to get more once a reading is done.

No Joke

It doesn't matter how long you have been working with your psychic abilities - - if you take your gift lightly, treat it as a joke, or allow your ego to get in the way of your work, your psychic abilities will decline.

Being psychic isn't just about you. You are the physical manifestation of a spiritual being. Your team - spirit guides, masters, angels, etc. - works with you to give you the information you need. Taking the work seriously is a sign to your spirit team that you respect them and their help. They like to be thanked and appreciated just as much as you do, so do it often.

If you treat your psychic ability as a joke or a party trick, you will find that the information you receive becomes less reliable. Your guides will step away from assisting you in psychic endeavors. This also applies to your ego. If you allow your ego to get involved, that is like slamming the door shut on your team.

Development Circle

One of the best ways to learn about psychic and medium abilities is to be part of a development circle. This is a group of like-minded individuals who come together regularly to learn about their psychic and medium abilities. While it is helpful to have an instructor who is skilled as a psychic or medium, it is not necessary. Having a class of students who are each willing to teach topics can prove to be as effective.

When working in a circle, all students involved need to have a dedication to the class. Everyone needs to be on time for each class, every week. If a student is going to be late, they understand they may be locked out of the class. By having a set time and place to work on your development, your guides, masters, and angels will be there to assist you with your growth.

When you start each class you should open with a group psychic protection. If desired, you can then do a meditation to help you center and focus your mind. This allows you to be in better contact with your guides. Move on to the learning part of the class, using your connection to your guides to develop and grow. When the class is complete make sure you protect your energy by closing your chakras and using your psychic protection again.

The Message Gets Through

Spirit has a funny way of getting needed information to us. Sometimes you will receive subtle tips while other times you are hit upside the head with a brick. This example is an experience that exemplifies the brick.

Due to my job, I missed my regular weekly development class. I had spent the previous Saturday giving readings at a local metaphysical store. At the end of the day, the owner and I struck up a conversation about different metaphysical topics. The owner, who is a very skilled medium, always has interesting insights. We discussed how time works on the Spirit Plane then moved on to different aspects of the Akashic Records. She felt I should learn how to read the Akashic Records and suggested a book that might be helpful. I purchased the book and proceeded to read it cover to cover.

The following week when I returned to my circle, my fellow classmates were excited to tell me about the information they had received the previous week. While working with the tipping table, their guides came in and advised them that our group needed to work on learning about the Akashic Records and how to read them. To top it off, they also received information about how time works on the Spirit

Plane and how it is different from time on the physical plane. In one week's time, in two separate ways, we all received the same important information from spirit.

When spirit is wishing you to have information, they will use whatever is that their disposal to get it to you. Pay attention to times when something keeps popping up in your life. This synchronicity is designed to alert us to things we need to pay attention to. Their message at times will be subtle so it might prove difficult to discern. Other times it will be coming at you from all directions. It is important to recognize it when noticed.

Psychic Dream Journal

Have you ever had a dream about an event before it happened? Strangely enough, you probably have and don't even realize it. The problem is that you can't remember every dream.

Get a notebook and pen and place them next to your bed. Set your alarm clock about 15 minutes earlier than when you would normally awaken. Now, when you wake up, take 15 minutes to write down the information about the dreams you just had. Don't forget to date your dream journal entries. As you write more and more, take a look back over past dreams and see if you recognize an occurrence of any dream coming true. Take note of when the event occurred and when the original dream was. This will help you determine how much time will elapse between current dreams and future events.

To better help you recall your dreams, before you go to sleep at night take your first and middle fingers and gently rub your "third eye." It is located in the center of your forehead, about an inch above where your nose and eyebrows meet. Ten seconds of rubbing in a circular fashion should be enough to activate it.

Astral Travel

Some dreams are so real that it feels like you were really there. There are "dreams" where this is actually the case! Astral travel allows your spirit to leave the body and to work on the energy side of our physical existence. You are still attached to our physical world as we know it, yet able to move about freely using your unconscious energy in a limitless way. You may travel great distances, see people you haven't seen in years or since their passing, and even see new and exciting places.

You can manage your astral travel by setting your intent before you go to sleep. As you lay down, bring up an image of the world in your mind. Pick a place you would like to go check out. Now, take your energy and lock into a specific place or person you have decided to visit. Hold those thoughts in your mind and drift off to sleep.

For example, you lay down and bring up the world. You decide you would like to go to Paris, France. So in your mind you locate where France is in the world. Then to help you get closer, you pick the energy of the Eiffel Tower to lock on to. Keeping these thoughts you drift off to sleep. During the night you will astral travel to the Eiffel Tower and Paris,

France. It may take you a few tries to have success with this, so don't give up if it doesn't work the first few times.

You may also wish to pick a destination that someone else can validate for you. For example, you have a friend who lives in San Diego, California. By choosing to astral travel there, your friend can validate the places you viewed. This will help you gain confidence in your ability.

So you know, time is not a limitation on astral travel. You can go backward or forward in time. You will not be able to change or alter events, but you will be able to see what was occurring at that time.

Crystals

Crystals can assist you with your development. Each crystal has a different energy and different purpose. Select crystals to help you based on your interests and goals. You can carry different crystals at the same time without worrying about them negating each other.

Many psychics and mediums will wear crystals as jewelry. You will discover that these stones are very beautiful and decorative and make for nice rings, necklaces, or earrings. You can also carry them in your pockets. Rather than lumping random crystals together in the same pocket, try laying them out and feeling how they work together. Then divide them up and carry them according to their desire.

I change my crystals out from time to time. This may be when I no longer need the benefits of a particular stone or I am recharging it. You will get a feel for when your crystals need a break the more you work with them.

To help your crystals work better for you, recharge their energy in the sun or moon. The choice of which you use is up to you. Go with the one you feel most connected to. Take 100% sea salt and sprinkle it on your crystal to cleanse it. Then put it into the sunlight or moonlight and allow it to charge. If you put it in the sunlight, only do so for a couple of hours max. For crystals that can fade in sunlight, you might wish to charge those in moonlight. Crystals can be exposed in moonlight all night. Don't forget to get them before the sun comes up. When recharging, you can put your crystals outside, in the natural light of the sun or moon. It is also safe to recharge them inside by putting them on a window sill where they will still get the sun or moonlight.

Auras

The aura is an electrical field that surrounds all living things. It is our personal electrical signature. You can use your aura to connect to anything else that has an aura. Once connected to that other aura, you can use that connection to discern information about the other being.

To connect to another person's aura is simple. First, find someone willing to let you make the connection. Second, with that person in close proximity (a few feet), expand your aura out and around the other person, enveloping them in your aura. Think of your aura as a blanket and you are under it, like a tent. Third, open up your psychic senses and determine information about this person. Last, when done, remove your aura and protect and ground yourself.

Once you understand how to do this over a few feet, you'll start to understand you can do it over greater distances as well. To connect over distance, you cannot wrap your aura over someone. Instead, take a strand of your aura, about the size of sewing thread, and extend it over the distance to the person you are reading. Do not be concerned that it is only thread size, it will work as effectively as using your full aura. Please remember your ethics, only connect to those who have given permission.

Seeing Auras

Humans, animals, and plants all have an auric field that surrounds each of them. Scientists have actually proven that the aura, or the energy field that surrounds a body, exists. While some see it naturally, it is a skill many psychics have learned.

Take a friend and place them about a foot from a white wall. Don't stare directly at them, but look about 2 inches above them. Between them and where you are looking, you will see a distortion. Usually when starting out you will only see this distortion about an inch or two from the surface of the person. If this is not yielding results, soften your gaze so your eyes are not fully in focus as you look above them.

Some see colors in the aura as soon as they start seeing the aura, but with others it takes practice. The colors found in the aura relate directly to the current energy, emotion, physical, or mental state of that person. It is possible to do a psychic reading from the auric colors.

Aura Cleanliness

The aura acts in part as a shield for us as well. If you performed the *Seeing Auras* exercise on someone, you may have also noticed little dark spots or even items in the aura. These are negative thought forms, either created by ourselves or directed at us by others.

It is important not to direct our anger or negative thoughts at others. Your negative thoughts can actually hurt others. Remember that thoughts are energy and negative energy will affect us. These thought forms stick to our auras and slowly drill their way into our physical bodies. Keeping your aura clean will assist you in having a higher energy vibration which facilitates your psychic work and development.

Negative self-thought or negativity directed at us by others damages our auras. This in turn weakens our natural ability to protect ourselves. As a result, we become sick. When you get in the shower or bath, take a minute to clean your aura as well. Ground yourself and use that positive energy to help clean out those dark spots and remove any negative attachments.

Using Your Energy With Your Aura

There are times and situations where you may feel a need to push your energy out so you can make better contact or even protect those around you. As an extrovert, I carry a very large aura. There are a few tricks to being able to push out and maintain a high energy focus.

Start by feeling where you normally carry your aura. You can have another person use dowsing rods to determine how far from your physical body. They hold the dowsing rods and slowly walk towards you. When the rods open, that is where your energy field starts. To expand your auric field think of pushing it out, like taking your hands and physically pushing it. Your first tries will only expand it a few feet. With practice, you will be able to expand it to an almost limitless distance.

If you are working to gain information, you don't need to push out your entire energy shell. Sending out a line or thread works just fine. It's your thought that determines how it works, so if you send out a single "high speed" line, you will discover it provides good information. This line can go long distances. I have connected to people in my city, in other states, and even outside of the country.

If you are in a situation where you feel you need to protect others, more energy is needed from you. First, you need to broaden your energy to cover everyone. You don't have to be in the middle of the group, just expand out the sides of your aura to cover them. Once you have established your safe zone, you need to do psychic protection to fill that area. You will need to concentrate on keeping your aura expanded while you do this. Once you have the protection in place, you can drop your aura back to its normal size. Generally, I would call it rude to do group protection without permission. However, I have encountered ghosts whose intent was very negative and the ghosts needed to be repelled.

Pendulums

One of the tools most associated with psychics is the pendulum. It is a very elegant item to use for divination work. While many psychics prefer to use ones that have a crystal as the weight, you can use just about any type of weight that is suspended from a string or chain. Should you wish to find one that has a crystal as the weight, look for one that resonates with you and try it out.

When you pick up a pendulum, you can ask it, "Are you my pendulum?" Watch what the pendulum does. If it does not respond, then this is not the one for you. If it responds in a crazy fashion, then this one is unable to handle your energy. When you find one that responds to you in a smooth way that is the pendulum for you.

Take your pendulum and wrap one end of the chain around your index finger. Next, hold the pendulum very still over the palm of your opposite hand. Ask the pendulum to show you a response for "no." The pendulum will respond by swinging. Now, ask the pendulum to show you a response for "yes." The pendulum will respond by swinging in a different direction. If you ask a question the pendulum doesn't understand or have an answer to, it will usually swing in a circle. The pendulum should sway no more than about an inch or two in its swing. If it is doing more than that, check the holding arm to make sure it isn't accidentally moving.

So, how exactly does a pendulum work? In essence, the pendulum receives information from you, the user. The answer is in you and your energy and vibration are what make the pendulum work. Basically, it is a physical manifestation of your psychic energy.

Dowsing Rods

Dowsing rods, or divining rods, are generally well known tools for finding water or minerals below the surface. They can also be used to detect your auric field and the presence of ghosts.

Take the shorter ends of the two "L" shaped rods in your hands. Do not grip them tightly, instead hold gently between your thumb, middle, and ring fingers. Take your index fingers and lightly touch the tips together. Next, position the long part of the rods so they form an "X" or as close to it as they will get. Don't allow the rods to be angled so one might interfere with the other, but so they will be level and able to move freely. Initially, the rods may swing back and forth a couple of times until they are adjusted to your energy. You are now ready to use the rods.

Think of your dowsing rods as "antennae" that feel for energy in your surroundings. Have someone move slowly toward you as you stand holding the rods. As they get closer, you will notice the rods swing open to a "V" formation. They are opening because they detected the energy in that person's aura. Try this with different people. You will notice that each person causes the rods to open at different distances from the holder. This is because different people keep their aura at different lengths from their bodies. Some keep their aura real close, while others extend theirs out by several feet. If you have someone who is really strong with their energy, you will find they can even open the rods from large distances.

Taking the dowsing rods ghost hunting works in the same fashion. The only risk here is that as you walk around focused on the rods you need to be careful not to trip and fall. Try to keep the rods in an "X" formation as you go from room to room. Should you enter a space where the rods open to the "V" formation, you have encountered a ghost.

Should you approach a large electrical source the rods will open. Take care that there are no outside electrical sources causing a false reading. If the dowsing rods are spinning like helicopter blades, this is user error. The rods should only open and close.

Psychometry

You have probably seen a TV show or movie where a psychic is holding an item and is able to give information about the owner of that item. Using the energy of an item to discern information about it or its owner is the skill of psychometry.

Start by rubbing your hands together in a circular motion. This will help activate the chakras in your hands and make you more receptive to receiving information. Hold the item in your hands and connect into its energy. Just go with what you feel, there are no wrong answers. To practice this, have an item from someone who can verify the information you get. This will help give you confidence in the ability. For best results, only use an item that is specific to its owner. Antiques will have the energy of different people and it will be harder to discern the energy of one person.

Billets – Take a piece of paper and have someone rub it between their hands for a minute or so. They have just put their energy on the paper and you can now do a reading for the person from it. They can also write their name or a question on the paper, thus providing a stronger connection to the individual. This will help you focus more on specific information the person is seeking.

Tarot

The tarot is an interesting tool. It can be difficult to learn because of the large number of cards and their meanings, as well as the different layouts you can use to perform a reading. It is a great tool for beginners and experts alike. You can spend a lifetime studying it and never feel you have completely mastered it.

When starting out, I suggest using the Rider-Waite deck. This is the most common deck and is the most written about as well. You will be able to find a great amount of information which will help you develop as a student of the tarot. As you start to give readings with the tarot, you will find there are certain cards whose meanings you feel are a little different from the definitions given. Follow your intuition here, a card in one reading may have a certain meaning and an entirely different one in the next.

Also, start out reading the cards in the upright position. It will be easier to learn only one set of definitions for the cards instead of two. Yes, the inverted card usually represents negative information. However, if bad news is going to come in, it will make itself known in the upright cards as well. Get a good handle on the cards in an upright position, then start working on their inversions.

Stick to the basic layouts for the cards and what each card means in its place. Learn 3 to 4 basic layouts. Start with a 3 or 5 card spread. They are easy to remember and can be used in many circumstances. The Celtic Cross and Tree of Life are two good deep layouts that provide a lot of information to a client. Remember, sometimes a one card pull is all a client needs. You don't need to overwhelm them with a Celtic Cross just to be fancy.

If you feel a need to create your own layout, by all means, do it. However, as a caution, try it out before taking it public. The cards will work with you and your intent. Coming up with your own spread is fine as long as it's not ego driven. The tarot is very adaptable as a tool of divination.

Making the Cards Come to Life

One of the hardest things for a beginning student to do with the tarot is to turn the layout into a reading. Each card in the spread has a position and a corresponding definition of what that spot represents. However, each card plays upon the card before it, after it, and often times near it in the spread.

The reading starts with a question by the client. Shuffle the cards while the client concentrates on the question. If you would like, you can know the question while you shuffle. Either way, this helps to set the intent for the deck as it prepares to be cut. You can read each card as you pull them or you can lay them all out to get the full picture, it's your choice. Start with the first card and explain each card that comes up and relate it back to the client's question. Then as each new card appears in the spread, connect it back to the one before it. You are building a chain with the cards that will show how decisions were made that led to where the client is currently and where he or she is going. Look into the cards and use your psychic abilities to pick up on why each card is important in its position and what the imagery on the card tells about the question.

Pay attention to the suit of each card. This will help you know if the client is focused on action (wands), emotion (cups), thought (swords), or money/home (pentacles). Use these in relation to where they sit in the spread to give you insight about your client. Utilize your psychic ability to look beyond the card and into how and why this card is relevant to the reading.

Ask the client to hold all additional questions until the end of the spread. Allowing the reading to be disrupted may confuse beginners and make the reading more difficult to complete. If the client offers any information during the reading, that is fine. Do not question the client during the reading.

It is not uncommon for the client to ask for clarification about a card after the reading. You have given them a lot of information and they may be overwhelmed. Answer their questions so they get the most out of the reading.

Runes

Runes are an ancient written language used by Germanic peoples as far back as the 2nd century AD. Modern rune divination stems from the Elder Futhark of 24 different symbols and the more recent addition of one blank. Each symbol has a different meaning and is interpreted by the rune master or psychic as the symbol relates to the question.

Runes are generally carved into round wooden discs, stones, crystals, or clay. When doing a reading, the psychic will have you pose your question and select your runes. Some psychics lay them out like a tarot reading, others just read them in the order pulled. There is no right or wrong way when doing this type of reading, it is up to the psychic to determine how they work best as a divination tool.

Scrying

Scrying is the ability to gaze into an item and view images as they appear. Popular items used for scrying are crystal balls, water, and mirrors. When attempting to gaze into any of these items in hopes of seeing images, there are a few techniques to help make it more successful.

Whatever object you use for scrying, do not stare directly onto the surface of the item. Rather, soften your gaze so the crystal, mirror, or water loses its 3-dimensional form and becomes 2-dimensional. You want to be able to look past the surface and into the item you are scrying with.

What is softening your gaze? You need to be able to take your eyes slightly out of focus. You don't want to stare with the intent of burning a hole in an item. As you soften your gaze, it allows your physical eyes to relax and take in images not only from the center, but from the periphery as well. The images you see will not be like a movie. You may get a horse, then an airplane, and lastly a color. What you see is relevant to your psychic mind.

When scrying you want to use very soft lighting. A candle or two is my preferred lighting as the flickering of the flame helps to reveal images in the medium you are using. The placement of the lighting is important as well. You want the candles out of your field of vision. Put them beside and behind you or slightly above you and behind you. Eyes are attracted to light and movement so keep them from being a distraction.

Scrying With a Crystal Ball - Getting the right crystal ball for scrying is very important. Natural quartz crystal is the easiest to learn with. Synthetic or acrylic are less desirable as these balls are clear and very hard to get energized to do this work. You can get large ones for a good price, but your scrying work will suffer as a result.

When shopping for your ball, don't just grab the first one you see. If at all possible see a few of them at once. You can get a feel for the energy of the ball and can determine which one you will like the most. If you do not have any new age type stores in your area, find a psychic fair or check for a local rock club or show.

Starting out, get the best crystal ball you can afford. Some people like working with a ball that has inclusions. Inclusions are imperfections in the ball, which look like cracks, chips, etc. The inside of my crystal ball also has a veil. The veil looks like a little spider web or a bunch of very small bubbles in the ball. The veil and inclusions allow for the reflection of light to create the images seen by the psychic mind.

When you look at the crystal ball, soften your gaze so you are not looking at the outside of the ball, but inside. When you get past the 3-dimensions of the ball, where you are seeing just the interior of the crystal, you are ready to scry. As the light flickers behind you, it will bounce off the inclusions, allowing you to see shapes and images. Don't expect images to just pop right out, this is a skill that takes time and practice to perfect.

Scrying With a Mirror - While any mirror will work for this skill, don't use one smaller than 12 inches. Lay the mirror on a flat surface where you can gaze down upon it at a 45-60 degree angle. As you look into the mirror, you should see the wall behind the mirror. You want to have a blank wall (any color, although white is preferred).

Again, put the candles behind or above and out of your field of vision. You want to soften your gaze as you look into the mirror so that you are no longer looking at the glass, but your gaze is caught inside the mirror. This is when you move past the 3 dimensions of the mirror. Clear you mind and allow whatever to appear. These visions are only for the viewer and will not be seen by others. Again, this is a skill that takes time and practice to develop.

Scrying With Water - When choosing a bowl to use for water scrying, find one that is large and flat. Make sure the bowl is one color on the inside. White, yellow, or black is preferred, but any will work. Make sure there are no textures or patterns in the bottom of the bowl. If you have one that smoothly transfers from the bottom into the walls, that works best.

Fill the bowl with about an inch of water. It doesn't need to be full, just enough to give the water a reflective property. You want to make sure the light you are using is high enough that it is able to get to the water inside the bowl.

Again, you want to soften your gaze and look into the water, not at the water surface. You need to move past the 3 dimensional physicality of the water to see the images. As with the other forms of scrying, it will take time and practice to perfect this technique.

Table Tipping

This is an amazing technique for contacting spirits. While this can be done by an individual, the energy is better if you can get 3-4 people to do this exercise. To give you the best chance of success, use a small, light, wooden table with a top that is wider than the legs.

Before you get started, make sure to use your psychic protection and work with your guides to invite only higher energies. Should someone wish to make contact with you, they can. You should not ask for or try to force individuals to come through. It takes a lot of energy for those who are in the spirit world to communicate this way. Accept their messages as a gift.

When you sit down, activate your palm chakras by rubbing your palms together in a circular motion. Then slightly cup your hands and place them very lightly so the palms are over the table. Do not lean or place weight over the table, allow the table to move freely of its own accord. It will do so. Playing upbeat music in the background is helpful as well. Also, try to raise the energy in the room by laughing.

Those on the spirit plane need to slow down their energy vibration in order to communicate. Help them out by speeding up your energy. Imagine a long funnel above yourself or your group. Take your energy and spin it up the tube as far as you can. This will allow the spirits to make the connection to your energy and help the table work.

When you are ready to start, ask aloud "Is there anyone in spirit here tonight that wishes to communicate with us? Please tip the table so we know you are here." You may need to restate this question a few times, pausing for a minute between to allow spirit to act. Once the table starts tipping, it is best to ask just "yes" and "no" questions when starting out. By this I mean if the table tips, the answer is "yes" and if the table does not tip, the answer is "no." For example, "if this is a family member, tip the table," or "if the spirit communicating with us is male, tip the table." Be specific in your questioning and how you ask spirit to respond. Confusing questions will cause spirit to stop.

Your responsibilities are to keep the energy in the room up so the spirit can work and to keep the questions simple so the spirit doesn't have to work hard. Trying to get the spirit to tip the table multiple times per answer is a waste of time and energy.

As your experience with table tipping grows, you will understand that spirits, guides, and angels move the table in different ways. My experience has shown that human spirits and guides move the table back and forth. However, higher angelic energies will move the table back and forth as well as rotate and slide the table.

Utilize all of your different clair abilities when using the table. Spirits, guides, masters, angels, and archangels come to provide messages that you will not know. Asking them to give information to you in an intuitive way will help you have a better table tipping session. Remember to trust it through when using the table.

When you finish working with the table, take time to thank those that came through. It takes a lot of energy from each side to make it work and being appreciative will help make future sessions better.

Ouija Boards

I'll make this simple, **_NO!!!!!_**

Here is why. Ouija boards invite unknown entities and ghosts into unsuspecting people's lives. Note, I'm not saying spirits, I'm using the words entities and ghosts very specifically. Entities are low level beings who are generally very negative in their actions. They do things like possessions, they do not leave when asked, they negatively influence the living, etc. Ghosts can act in the same fashion; not all do, but they can. The vast majority of people who use Ouija boards are not trained in how to use them safely. Kids think it's a silly game and it's not real. Because kids have a natural higher energy, they easily attract bad entities and ghosts when using a Ouija board. Also, kids don't know anything about psychic protection and defending against possession, which makes them perfect targets for these lower entities and ghosts.

When untrained users sit down with a Ouija board and start to play, they open up a door to entities and ghosts who would otherwise not be interested. These negative energies then have a passageway to the people using the board because they have surrendered their energy to help whatever come through. After having a Ouija board session, these entities hang around causing trouble, anything from hauntings to possessions. Not a good result from just playing a "game." Go play Monopoly® or Scrabble® instead.

There are skilled psychics and mediums who do have the required knowledge and ability to use a Ouija board in a safe and productive manner. If you really have to use one, *please* have someone who is knowledgeable in the proper use of a Ouija board help you.

Psychic Games

If you are wanting to work on your abilities alone or do not have a development circle that you can work with, playing psychic games can be beneficial. The purpose of playing the games is to strengthen your psychic abilities. The more you are able to accurately foresee events before they occur, the more confident you will be in using your gift.

Try the following games using your strongest "clair." Should you wish, you can also use these techniques to help develop your weaker "clairs." Use these games as guidelines to help you strengthen your specific skills.

Because you are playing them alone, you cannot lie to yourself or give yourself credit when it is not due. Remember, you cannot ethically invade anybody's private information. These games are designed to help build your psychic muscle without crossing that line. Keep your ego out of the games, play them honestly and you will grow.

Psychic DJ - Turn on a favorite radio station. If possible, try to catch it mid-song. Your goal is to determine something about the next song. It can be something as simple as male or female singer, or is it a slow or fast song. It can also be difficult like artist name or song title. You want to avoid hearing anything about upcoming songs by the DJ.

Take your energy and move into the radio and follow the energy back to the station. When there, get a feel for the room. Take a look at the computer screen and psychically determine what song is next. Take the information you feel and note it about the next song. If what you picked up on was not part of the next song, wait a few songs to see if it plays out. Just because you're off by a song or two, doesn't mean it's a miss, it means your psychic pick up is delayed. This will help you to refocus to be more accurate.

Here are a couple of examples. You reach out and get that the next song is by a woman. The next song is by a long haired male artist and then the following song is by a woman. Were you thrown off by the man's long hair? Since the second song is performed by a woman, you need to refocus your energy a little more. Not a direct hit, but a learning experience.

Let's say you feel the next artist is going to be Elton John. However, the next song is by The Who and it is "Pinball Wizard." Well, in the rock opera "Tommy," Elton John played the role of the Pinball Wizard. This would be a hit.

Psychic Television - So, you're sitting around watching television, what a great time to work on your psychic abilities. Obviously, you know the program you are watching but you don't know what the next commercial is going to be. You will have 4-8 commercials on each break so it's a great opportunity to flex your psychic muscles.

Reach out with your energy again and feel the energy back to the station. Get a feel of what commercials may be coming up. You can start out by picking up general information about the commercials. As you develop your psychic abilities, you can pick up products, or possibly celebrity endorsements.

You reach out and feel the next commercial will be a car commercial. The product in the commercial is for real estate, but there is a car in the background. This would be a miss because the car was not a focus of the ad. Should they be driving around in the car or if the car is the centerpiece of the commercial, that would be a hit. Don't forget to see if the car ad appears as a following commercial.

Psychic People Watching - Set yourself up around a blind corner where you are unable to view the people about to walk into view. Reach around the corner with your energy and pick up on who will be coming around the corner next. When you start, just work on picking up simple stuff like man, woman, or child. As you develop, you can add in details like clothing, jewelry, and accessories.

This exercise requires the most honesty in determining what you are receiving and what actually occurs. If you are discerning a man, and a woman with short hair comes around the corner, it's a miss. Still, keep track of the next person. When you decide to step it up, it can get difficult. This is where your honesty will help you develop. If you are going for specifics, you have to stick with them. If you believe there are gold hoop earrings and its only gold studs, that's a miss. Determining clothing can be tricky as well. Do you see blue? Well, of course, lots of people wear jeans. Try to be as specific and get as much detail as you can.

Do not let your ego gain control of the process. Your ego will tell you that your information was correct when it really was not. Ego is the enemy of psychic ability and growth. Be honest -- in the end you will be better for it.

The Future

Your future in developing your psychic abilities is up to you. This is not an overnight process and may take years to develop into a strong working skill. You will also discover there are many different areas in which you wish to learn and grow. The information I've shared with you will be a handy reference when you encounter blockages or need some additional insight. Always be a student and keep learning! I wish you the best as you continue to discover your talents.

About the Author

CB Bjork is a psychic, medium, author, Reiki master, teacher, and public speaker. He has appeared as a guest on radio and television shows. His classes on psychic development are highly regarded by students as educational and helpful.

CB has a unique gift for bringing the tarot to life. His informative and direct reading style is appreciated by his clients. Through using the Akashic Records, he has been able to assist many by understanding their past lives and how they affect their current life. He enjoys performing mediumship platform work for groups and events.

You can learn more about CB by visiting his website, cbbjork.com. You can also find him at Facebook.com/cbpsychic.

NOTES:

NOTES:

Made in the USA
Middletown, DE
25 March 2016